ADVANCE PRAISE FOR *BACK TO SC*　*ROWNUPS*

Your book is amazing at.

—Barbara M. Jones,　　　　　Studies in Education,
University of Illino.　　　　　national Consultant

What a treat! Besides your ability to write in a very conversational "coach-at-your-elbow" style, this book has the ring of personal experience and authenticity that is impossible to fake. The power of your writing to become a personal runs through everything you have

—Donald G. Kelsey, Libra:
Learner

This is an important book for anyone mature enough to know that the need to learn is a lifelong practice—a commitment to grow beyond artificial deadlines set up by the unenlightened. *Back to School for Grownups* provides the stories and steps just right for our time.

—Marika and Howard Stone; Co-authors, *Too Young to Retire: 101 Ways to Start the Rest of Your Life*

There is no stopping someor encouraged me to do the bes enough. I never knew how g encouraging words!

—Kathy Waldo, Inver

This is a great guide or hand a career—young, mid-career it's honest; you point out the about options.

—Janene Connelly, Fa

# BACK TO SCHOOL FOR GROWNUPS:
## YOUR GUIDE TO MAKING SOUND DECISIONS

(And How to Not Get Run Over by the School Bus)

Laura H. Gilbert, PhD

ISBN 1-449551653

EAN-13 9781449551650

For Arius and Avery,
who provided perspective and study rocks
when Grandma went back to school.
&
To my friend and mentor
Jacki Keagy,
who spent her lifetime helping others achieve their dreams.

# Acknowledgments

This book would not have happened without the support and encouragement of my friend and mentor, Cheryl Leitschuh, EdD, who steadfastly believed in this project through several stops and starts. Thanks for your patient enthusiasm, wise counsel, and hours of engaged listening.

Thanks to friends and family for asking how the book was going and staying to hear the answer. Special thanks to Alex M. Liuzzi, who walked his mother through the publishing process when his own first novel went to press.

Thanks to Suzy Bergstrom, Stacey Bellows, Janene Connelly, Sandra Forslund, Jeff Hemminger, Donald Kelsey, Alison Killeen, Meilin Obinata, Richard Caylor, Tamara Markus, Anna Short, Linda Stone and Lori Weise-Parks, who contributed time and expertise in support of this project. And special thanks to my editors Christy Barker and Kristen Gandrow, whose keen eyes, patience, and attention to detail are greatly appreciated, and to Lori Peterson who deserves full credit for the subtitle and all the smiles that come with it.

Thanks to the many higher education professionals who shared their insights and enthusiasm for adult learners through our conversations and the Higher Education Professionals Survey. Special thanks to Dr. Reatha Clark King, former president of Metropolitan State University, who handed me my first back-to-school diploma many years ago.

Finally, special thanks to the adult students who took time from their hyper-busy schedules to share their back-to-school stories. Your words will continue to inspire and encourage others long after your own journey is complete. Thank you!

# Table of Contents

# Introduction

*Back to School for Grownups* is a practical guide for the adult who is contemplating a return to the classroom. Whether you are considering a certificate program or a PhD—or completely unsure which road to take—this book contains information to help you make the best decisions *for you*.

Based on the real-world, practical experience of adults who have successfully taken this journey, *Back to School for Grownups* goes beyond typical self-help books. *Back to School for Grownups* explores important but rarely addressed questions on the minds of many returning adult students such as, "Am I too old to be a ___?" "Is it worth it?" "Can I afford it?" "Where do I begin to explore options?" and "Do I have what it takes to succeed as an adult student?" In addition to the author's perspective, the book includes insights from adults who returned to school and provides complete results of the Higher Education Professionals Survey conducted exclusively for this edition.

Returning to school is a big decision and a big but do-able project. Experience teaches us that big decisions and big projects have the best outcome when preceded by careful planning. Thus, the bulk of this book helps the reader establish a solid foundation on which a return to school can be securely built. The second half of the book includes practical advice on how to enjoy the journey and make a successful leap to a new (or enhanced) field of endeavor.

*Chapter One*, "Time to Regroup," gives a special nod to Baby Boomers who are entertaining thoughts of returning to school. Perhaps you were laid off last week, or your last child graduated, or a friend is returning to school. If you are wondering "What now?" (or, "What happened?") Chapter One has something for you! This chapter offers insight into often-overlooked subtleties that can block a journey before it begins. By the end of this book's first chapter, you will be equipped to answer the question, "Is an educational journey right for me?"

*Chapter Two*, "A Journey Considered," explores common next questions:

- Is this the best time for me to return to school?
- Can I succeed as a student?
- How do I decide what to study?
- Am I too old for a career as a ___?
- And the ultimate question: Is it worth it?

*Chapter Three*, "It Really Is All About You," digs into the personal and financial details of returning to school. A three-step process points the career-changing reader toward a wise, personal educational choice. Ten questions encourage healthy educational investment decisions, and a chart is included to track your finances along the way.

*Chapter Four*, "Going Back to School," describes the multitude of educational models open to today's students and how to choose the best one for you. Key aspects of the admissions process are highlighted, with pointers to help you get into the program you want. The chapter ends with tips on how to psyche yourself up for the first day of class.

*Chapter Five*, "Enjoying the Journey," offers simple suggestions to make your school days memorable (in a good way). Chapter Six, "Making the Leap," suggests ideas that career-changers can implement for a successful transition to their next endeavor.

*Chapter Seven* closes this edition of *Back to School for Grownups* with real-life stories from individuals from many walks of life who also returned to school and succeeded. You can, too!

An Appendix provides the complete results of the Higher Education Professionals Survey conducted exclusively for this edition. Deans, professors, and an array of administrators responded to the following questions:

1. Have you seen an increase in the number of adults returning to school? Why or why not?

2. What are the three most common characteristics of successful adult students?

3. What are the three most common derailers for adult students?

4. What one thing should adult students returning to school know?

Their responses provide insight and a view of adult learners from the other side of the desk.

The quotes that begin each chapter came from survey respondents and Travel Story writers.

Visit the Back to School for Grownups website for a variety of tools, articles and resources for your journey. (Check the last printed page of this book for a code you can use to download many of the charts presented in the book!)

Enjoy!

Laura
November 2009
http://backtoschoolforgrownups.com
laura@backtoschoolforgrownups.com

"Adult learners are capable of much more
than they imagine."
Higher Education Survey Respondent

# CHAPTER ONE

## TIME TO REGROUP

*"The nature of work today demands
new skills and knowledge."*

"Get your degree in eighteen months, one night a week."
"President encourages moms to return to school." "$12 billion proposed for expansion of community college programs for working adults." "Workforce programs increase available funds for retraining." Everywhere you look there are stories of adults returning to school. Billboards, radio ads, web pop-ups, and more display happy graduates who finished their degree, found their dream job, or advanced their career through additional education. Even a local bus stop ad blasted the age argument with a cap-and-gown photo of ninety-five-year-old Nola Ochs, the world's oldest person to receive a college degree. In response to unrelenting layoffs, job outsourcing, and predictions of multiple careers in one's lifetime, co-workers, friends, and relatives are returning to school in record numbers. Some seek to fulfill a lifelong dream while many view additional education as a requirement for economic survival.

Are you thinking about returning to school but also wondering how we even got here? Would you pay good money for an accurate "you are here" sign in your life right now? If so, then Chapter One is for you. Following a brief discussion of changes to the work environment, this chapter takes a look at influential shifts in recent decades that have played a role in how we see ourselves in the world of work and careers. Readers from the Baby Boomer generation lived through these shifts. The second half of Chapter One explores the effects of these shifts on 1) change, 2) resources available for dialogue and support, and 3) the legacy we might leave for generations that follow.

## NOT YOUR FATHER'S WORK ENVIRONMENT

While many of us were busy building careers that we expected would last a lifetime, things changed—really changed. For starters, think about changes to the basic model for finding a job. Unlike today's global, internet-based, networking-rich job searches, several generations of people and jobs paired up in pretty much the same way. Companies sought workers who could build products. In exchange, workers expected companies to provide the means of survival for themselves and their families. Job openings were announced. People responded. Selections were made on clear and commonly understood criteria—whether the ad was as broad as "Man—must be hard worker," or as specific as "Accountant—3 years experience with VisiCalc in manufacturing environment."

Roles and rules were equally understood: work hard, be honest, don't step on any toes, and you are likely to have lifetime employment. Virtue was found by receiving a day's pay for a day's work and thus providing for one's family. If employee and employer each did his part, everything was hunky dory. To leave a steady job raised questions about one's personality or sense of responsibility. Stability meant success. Change meant danger.

Is there any wonder our elders respond with worry, confusion, and long lists of "just do _____" when we share news of the latest downsizing, merger, or outsourcing event that has us once again looking for work? Their well-learned fear, appropriate for their time, may produce a stream of woulda, coulda, shoulda's from those we hoped would offer comfort in tough times. Unfortunately, this implication of control can be a rather heavy burden when some faceless leadership team outsources our department to China.

Does anyone really believe our input was requested and we messed up the answer? Or our position was eliminated because we didn't work hard enough, or annoyed someone like we used to irritate our little sister? Actually, deep down, the answer is probably yes. In an earlier time, this was often an accurate assumption. In today's environment, an elder's wisdom about life in general may be extremely useful while his or her perception about our work world may be less than accurate. Our fast-changing, global, internet economy still requires employees to crunch the numbers, treat the sick, and drive the bus—but while also inventing new ways to work, be productive, and succeed. In exchange, today's employees expect more than a paycheck. They want to make a difference, find meaning, fulfill a purpose.

Many of us hardly recognize the world when compared to the one we pictured peering forward from our youth. More common is a perplexed, "What happened?" or, "Wow! I never imagined I'd be doing this right now." Traditionally, middle age was a time to review one's achievements, send the kids off to discover their own lives, go after the last big promotion, and then wind down toward retirement (starting with the purchase of a red sports car, of course).

Today, a different picture has emerged. For many, middle age has become a time to regroup, retrain, and find one's third or fourth or fifth wind or, as Billy Crystal's character in the 1980s film *City Slickers* said, embrace a "do-over." Whether by choice or mandate, this "do-over" time can be exhilarating—the proverbial opportunity to start again while equipped with one's experience, knowledge, and wisdom.

The next section highlights influential shifts that occurred within many homes during recent decades. These internal shifts have played a significant role in how careers are built today. This is not meant to be an exhaustive list or even a "most-critical" list. For example, two of the most significant shifts that have affected corporations—globalization and outsourcing—are only discussed within the context of narrower shifts that demand an individual choice. Likewise, historical and sociological details are left for the work of experts in those fields. The intent is simply to present a glimpse into several subtle (and not so subtle) changes that have had a profound impact on the role and natural life of work.

# INFLUENTIAL SHIFTS

## From One to Two Careers Per Household

Historians may differ as to the precise decade in which American households made the shift from one adult per household in paid employment to two. The tremendous changes involved in this process have affected many people in today's workforce. Although this shift led to positive change for individuals and employers, the process of getting there included a fair amount of confusing expectations, conflicting personal messages and changing definitions of success. Individuals born between 1946 and 1964—the baby boomer generation—witnessed the entire transition. Born into one career households, baby boomers were the first generation forced to choose which path to take. Should they follow the traditional path of their parents and grandparents or set out on a new path of equal rights in the workplace and the kitchen?

As young adults, many baby boomer women struggled to make family and career choices not available to generations of women before them. Strong opinions from both genders were in ample supply, each viewpoint implying dire consequences for women who followed the "other" path. Should she stay home and be a traditional mom and wife per the June Cleaver model of *Leave it to Beaver* fame? Was she a better wife and mother if she took a nonthreatening (to her husband) part-time job for "pin money" that still gave her enough time to keep up the house, raise well-mannered kids, and have dinner on the table by five? Should she burn her bra and be a free spirit? Or should she hit the books, abandon the wife/mother role, and become a "career woman?"

Eventually the image of "superwoman" emerged as the model for the fully-actualized woman. Do it all or you were missing out on something necessary to be satisfied, happy, and whole. At least, that was the message. Best symbolized in a mid-1970s Enjoli perfume commercial, a sexy blonde in a business suit swings a frying pan to a stripper beat over the lyrics, "I can bring home the bacon...fry it up in a pan...and never let you forget you're a man, 'cause I'm a WOMAN...with Enjoli...the new 8-hour perfume for the 24-hour woman." Those of us who tried this model soon realized 1) it wasn't the same without a backup band and voice-over, 2) no one looks that good without a director, and 3) the math was just plain wrong, as twenty-four hours weren't nearly enough.

No matter what road she chose, there was another not taken. Consequently, baby boomer women who return to school are often exploring a new path. The career housewife may be exploring educational options in order to acquire her first job outside the home. If she balanced household responsibilities with volunteer activities and low-key part-time jobs, she may be returning to school to pursue the first paid occupation she views as a full-fledged career. Women who have worked full-time for twenty or thirty years may view going back to school as an opportunity to pursue a career that was less accessible to women the first time around. And, yes, a few baby boomer women pursue additional education purely for fun and self-fulfillment.

Likewise, baby boomer men have experienced a lifetime of shifting roles. A man's proper role as provider, husband, and parent handed down from his father, grandfather and generations of grandfathers before him, has been attacked, revered, and attacked again. Once-honorable behavior such as opening the door for a woman suddenly became suspect. In order to be a good husband to his working wife, he was expected to embrace household tasks likely categorized as "women's work" in his childhood home. I can only imagine that baby boomer men must sometimes feel as though every day is another spin of the game show wheel to see who they are supposed to be today. Add to this mix the workforce entrance of capable, confident, women determined to break the glass ceiling supported by gender-discrimination rules and it is understandable how the image of living in a cave with a keg and a group of guys may start to sound appealing. At the same time, as with their female peers, baby boomer men have new options to pursue interests put aside by early roles and responsibilities. For more than two decades, two insightful men, Richard N. Bolles (*What Color is Your Parachute*) and Richard Leider (*Living on Purpose*), along with others led the way for both genders to look beyond the paycheck when making career choices. In response, educational institutions have seen an increase in male applicants for programs in nursing, elementary education, and social service, particularly among men returning to school.

Baby boomer couples who successfully paved the dual career path may find midlife to be a good time to make a change. This isn't always a shared feeling. If both partners have well-established careers and one partner begins to contemplate a change in pursuit of a lifelong goal or dream, he/she may face a "don't rock the boat" stance from a nervous partner. A perceived place of security can feel more comfortable than the pursuit of an unknown path. However, this is a wonderful time for reflection and growth as topics such as purpose, personal goals, occupational contribution to community, and legacy are explored individually and as a family.

## From One House/Home to Many

Shifts in geographical living patterns also influence current options for educational program selection. Think back to your childhood. How often did you move? How often did your parents move as children? Unless your family is new to the U.S., your parents may have grown up in what became known as "the family home" (or the family farm). As newlyweds in the forties, fifties, sixties and seventies, your folks probably worked long and hard to purchase a family home of their own in which you grew up.

Unless your father was in the military or climbing a corporate ladder built by relocations, many returning adult students have one physical structure that comes to mind when recalling the home of their youth. Residential moves were typically initiated by one's long-time employer. A self-initiated relocation, similar to self-initiated job change, implied that a family structure may be unstable or otherwise in trouble. Again, the underlying message was: obey the boss and you'll live happily ever after. Status quo equals safety; change equals danger.

Today, few people purchase a house intending to pass it on to the next generation. Homes are bought and sold (or rented) as a place to live during this job, or so the kids can attend that school, or until the next adventure comes along. Consequently, today's adult returning to school may have the geographic freedom and social support to attend a specialized academic program in another state or country (or the program that offers the best grant money).

Well-intentioned elder relatives still living in the family home (literally or figuratively) may find it difficult to understand why one would want to do such a thing or, more importantly, how it could possibly be a good idea. In contrast, consider the geographic perspective for home and careers of those born after 1970. These are the young executives to whom you will be looking for a fresh start—whether or not you could have been their babysitter.

## From Limited to Limitless Choices

Baby boomers have truly witnessed the information explosion, and with it the amount of information available to discover career options. In earlier years, information about specific careers was limited, in part because career choices were viewed narrowly through the lens of race, religion, nationality, and gender. Young single women had three standard career options: secretary, nurse, or teacher. Early laws required women to resign from certain jobs when they married and from other jobs when they were seven months pregnant. Men often followed their fathers into a family business.

Questions about certain careers were posed to those who worked in the profession or, more often, those who knew someone who did ("I think my cousin's sister-in-law's neighbor is a _____"). Information about emerging career opportunities was limited by the savvyness of the school guidance counselor (who, in all fairness, was subject to the same limited information sources—while also coaching volleyball). Consequently, one's career options were drawn primarily from well-intentioned family members and teachers, each more interested in graduating responsible citizens than helping students "find themselves." Within the limited options before them, baby boomers were encouraged to choose an honorable, steady job they believed they could do well with perseverance and hard work; for men, ideally one with promotion opportunities or a ladder to climb. Special talents, individual personality, or personal interests were secondary considerations. Success depended on one's efforts to work hard, follow orders, be loyal, and overcome personal weaknesses. Career success was defined in tangible factors such as salary, promotion, and receipt of the gold watch at retirement.

Today's approach to careers is reversed. Start with who you "are" and then look for a career match. Raised with computer technology Generations X and Y (or, the "Millennials") grew up with increased access to information about careers and the best-match personalities. New models of child psychology celebrated individuality and delivered the message that all options were open to everyone. Posters of role model "firsts" covered school walls encouraging children to reach for their own dreams as had the first woman astronaut, the first Hmong dentist in America, and the first African American CEO of a Fortune 500 company. Talent development programs and career exploration curricula started in preschool and continued through corporate orientation. As these generations entered the workforce, new philosophies claimed that the secret to success was found by enhancing one's strengths and not worrying as much about improving weaknesses. Discover and embrace your true self and you will go far and be happy. While the concept of success still includes a monetary component, true success is viewed as including work/life balance, personal fulfillment, and living the life one wants to live.

In short, recent generations have been encouraged to use who they *are* in order to become who they *want to be, today*—knowing the latter will likely change over time. The immovable core is one's self and all that entails. Key questions include: "Who am I?" "What do I like to do?" "What has meaning for me?" and "what are my talents?"

In contrast, the baby boomers were encouraged to identify *who they sought to become, for their lifetime,* and then *apply themselves* to make it happen. The initial career decision was the immovable core around which everything else adjusted. Success was viewed as entirely in their hands, based on their ability to work hard, do what the boss said, and not rock the boat. The key question was, "Can I work hard enough to successfully do the work?"

If you were raised under the baby boomer model and are considering a career change, be prepared to explore new questions geared toward knowing oneself. Today success is often viewed as a secondary outcome that follows a clear understanding of one's talents, strengths, innate personality, and dreams. This can be a stark, albeit welcome, contrast to the formula on which many of our first careers were built, where success was perceived as dependent on our ability to apply ourselves through a strong work ethic in order to make our vision happen. The opportunity to explore one's talents, personality, and choices is often exhilarating. Figuring out how to do this for the first time at age forty, fifty, or sixty can be overwhelming. Not only does it shine a light on one's very essence, but with decades of experience, there is so much more essence to explore.

Today there is no end to the information one can collect about careers, career selection, and personal traits that allegedly spell success. This is the good news and the bad news. Limitless amounts of information can be worse than no information unless there is a surefire system to whittle it down to a manageable and personally accurate set —which there is not. Available resources tackle certain aspects of this task such as resume writing, interviewing, naming areas of job growth or salary, or matching one's traits with position titles. Compared to the limited information available to make our first career selection, midlife career changers can find themselves overwhelmed, feeling unable to get their arms around the information necessary to make the next career decision. Add the new emphasis on who we are deep down inside and the pursuit of a second career can be a downright bummer at times.

If this feels familiar, don't despair! We are blessed with brilliant leaders in this field whose writings, programs, and personal inspiration have resulted in myriad resources and opportunities to engage with other travelers along this path. Prime examples include Richard Leider's Working on Purpose™ program, Howard and Marika Stone's *Too Young to Retire*, and Richard Bolles' *What Color is Your Parachute—For Retirement*. For more personal attention, seek out top notch personal coaches who are experts at helping individuals uncover their strengths and true calling. If you prefer social interaction, look for networking groups such as *Shift*, where mid-career individuals discuss "encore careers" that add meaning to life and work.

However, watch out for the navel-gazing trap. Self exploration can become a black hole of wonderings and contemplation. To use a different metaphor, it can become the bright shiny thing that hypnotically draws one's attention away from the task at hand. Self knowledge is only one component of career selection. Learn what you can about yourself through a reasonable amount of time and effort, and then move forward. You can always continue self exploration along the way.

## From One Career to Many

By the late 1990s, labor and employment pundits were predicting the average American worker would have three to seven distinct careers during his/her lifetime. Unsettling layoffs, position outsourcing, and job obsolescence continue to send adults back to school each year to retool. Add the number of individuals changing careers out of personal choice and we have several strong indications that the data are true.

The prospect of multiple careers can be overwhelming, especially to those who dedicated their early adult lives to the success of a first occupation they believed would last until retirement. While younger generations may view multiple careers as an adventure, baby boomers are more apt to feel the rug was pulled out from under them. The middle-aged baby boomer whose career has just gone the way of the buggy whip may feel crushed by practical and personal concerns—"I don't have enough time (or energy) to start over!" "It has been decades since I was in school!" "What job will I be good at (or enjoy, or get paid enough to live on, or be hired for)?" or "What career will be secure?"

Many people faced with unexpected career change feel lost, not in a hopeless way but in a "Where *am* I?" kind of way, like waking up in the fifth hotel during a six-day road trip. Job and career change can contribute to stress, depression, and anxiety. If you are concerned about your emotional well being, you are not alone. Reach out. Join a job support group. Don't hesitate to seek professional help.

Likewise, a spouse who does not work outside the home may have similar concerns. This can be a time for relationship renewal as dreams, goals, and work-sharing options are reconsidered. Perhaps the stay-at-home spouse is eager to complete a degree program and return to the workplace. Maybe the wage-earner is ready to tend the garden, learn to cook, and drive the kids around. The oldest child might even be considering a college that offers deep discounts for parent/child pairs in attendance. Those who take a moment to recall their earliest couple conversations about work-related ideals may uncover new opportunities to reinvent themselves or get back on track to achieve personal goals.

Today it is possible to have multiple careers as diverse as wait staff, accountant, plumber, and research scientist. Yet many individuals choose to build new careers on top of core skills, experiences, and interests. Finding these tangential careers may take some brainstorming but, as the saying goes, they are often hidden in plain sight. What do you do in your free time (or used to do in younger days)? How do friends, co-workers, and family describe you? Observe your reactions to day-to-day events and experiences. What draws your attention? Do any themes emerge?

Several years ago I led an informal job group of senior executives, PhD scientists, and a veterinarian. Each individual held credentials from top educational institutions. The resumes vividly reflected professional achievements. Up to this point, their typical work week included fending off executive recruiters who waved attractive job offers from competitors. When we began, each of these highly-employable individuals was unemployed, most for the first time since joining the workforce decades earlier. Several spent the first weeks after job loss in relative seclusion simply to rest up and prepare for the onslaught of offers that had always come before—but were now alarmingly absent.

Their world had changed. Week after week, shock, confusion, questions of personal failure, and fear permeated the room. Efforts to seek comparable positions for which they were highly qualified failed to produce results. Pressure from spouses increased as they, too, wondered why this stellar professional was not yet bringing home a paycheck. We pressed on.

The critical breakthrough came the day one member raised the question, "What if things really *have* changed? What do we do now?" By temporarily suspending their reliance on the known model of the past, they decided to give creative thinking a chance. It couldn't hurt. They soon discovered that their traditional focus on title, money, and typical career progression had limited their thinking for themselves and each other. They still wanted these things, but the way to achieve them had changed.

The world was now open. Immediately ideas began flowing. Creative possibilities tangential to their prior positions were uncovered. Values and "must-haves" were clarified. Unappreciated personal talents emerged as key opportunities. A news article shared by one member led another to law school. During a conversation about second language skills, a former marketing director casually mentioned he had lived in Japan for a year as a high school exchange student. Although he had overlooked his twenty-years-dormant language talent, the group jumped all over it. He left the meeting armed with strong encouragement and our collective list of fast, free, or low-cost language programs to brush up his skills. A few weeks later he was the first of the group to land a new position—taking his marketing expertise into a role as Assistant Director of Asia Pacific Markets for a Fortune 500 company. Although this was a step back from his prior title and salary, the move opened new pathways that have since taken him far beyond his former roles.

Within the weeks that ensued, every member of the group landed employment. The prospective law student negotiated tuition reimbursement as part of his new position. Each individual was on a new career path built on the foundation of prior experience, but expressing their talents in new ways.

There is hope. There are opportunities. Start from wherever you are and build a path to the next career.

## CHANGE PERSPECTIVES

Are you tired of hearing about change? Acknowledging change. Accepting change. Managing change. Thriving in change. Embracing change. Consider this: if by definition "change" implies moving *from* one stable state *to* another stable state, as in changing from a seedling into an oak; or from a philosophy major to a math major; or from being a Pepsi drinker to a Coke drinker, can we safely assume a stable state is in our near future? Or has "change" become its own oxymoron indicating a stable state of constant flux?

If this were true, even the most flexible and adventurous among us would ultimately burn out. It simply isn't reasonable to expect one to be a master carpenter one year, heart surgeon the next, jazz musician the next, and so forth. Even with the talent for all three professions, there is neither the time to train and gain the requisite experience nor the time to build the professional connections, personal reputation, and a convincing story to earn top prizes in career after career after career. However, if one looks more broadly at one's goals in the context of a lifetime it is possible to be proficient and employed in any number of careers.

On the other hand, what happens to our psyche when we are told to get used to change as a constant? To learn to live with it? A few individuals will respond with excitement at the endless possibilities, probably the same people who love amusement park thrill rides. The rest of us may feel overwhelmed, unsure of where to begin, and whether the speculative outcome warrants the effort.

Embracing change that appears to be headed toward a clear and stable end is one thing; constant change with no end in sight leaves us exhausted, wondering how we will know when we're "done." Even the biggest roller coaster on earth has a start and an end. Like riding a roller coaster stuck in the "on" position, the thought of perpetual career change for the remainder of our years can make us queasy and stressed, wondering how we will be able to cope long term without an opportunity to stop and regain our balance.

The good news is that we can stop or at least pause. Consider the extended-journey traveler for whom stops along the way (planned or not) have the potential to provide moments of stability, rest, and great discovery. Look for places to pause and reflect on how far you've come along your own path. Identify milestones that will inform you where you are along this path. Give yourself credit for making each change that is necessary to get from where you are to where you want to be. Psychologically, and financially if possible, allow some flexibility for side trips and setbacks.

Remember, change is almost always possible if you take, as they say, one step at a time. By viewing each step in turn as a mini "end," it is possible to recapture the energy, focus, and perspective essential for the next leg of the journey.

One example comes from a large organization known for shifting people's positions nearly every six months. Rather than taking the outdated six-month standard to get fully acclimated to each new job, these employees take about six weeks. Sure, they miss some of the details, but applying the popular 80/20 rule, they glean 80% of the essence of the new job in 20% of the time. No one really worries about the rest. And based on the continuous success of this company, 80% is enough.

Most importantly, these individuals see position changes as part of an extended career journey—a journey that began with entrance into the workforce and will end somewhere at an unknown future date. They are simply travelers and observers on a journey called work. While many of their careers were launched with a specific vision in mind, they are flexible about where that vision leads. Because they don't worry about how long they remain in any one role, these individuals are open to career paths they didn't consider when they started out.

They are masters in the art of letting go when unfinished projects are replaced by new initiatives. Continuing education and lifelong learning are assumed. As long as they are challenged, rewarded, and paid, they are content. Rather than perceiving the changes as never-ending, each change presents an unexplored path. These individuals have learned to trust the journey.

## MAKING A GOOD DECISION

Chances are, by this point in life you have one or more individuals from whom you seek input or reassurance when faced with a significant challenge. Spouse, friends, co-workers, religious leaders, siblings, and adult children can offer insight and perspective. Parents, living or passed on, continue to play their part as the adult child wonders, "What would Mom/Dad say?" We may implicitly trust one or more of these individuals to encourage us to go the extra mile toward a worthy goal, and tell us the hard truth when we are about to make a poor decision.

Yet returning to school may touch on the hopes and dreams of others. Sometimes this feels initially like push-back from a spouse who is otherwise supportive of one's career choices. Any number of issues can be the cause, including discomfort with the current situation, fear of change, or jealousy of the opportunity to return to school. Plus, if the spouse's career has been fairly steady (paid or volunteer, in-home or outside the house), watching a partner embark on a new occupational adventure may raise concerns about the stability of the spouse's career. Further, if your career change is self-initiated and you are over forty, there may be encouragement to "just hold on for X more years and we can retire." Unfortunately, while many of us would have preferred that option, it is not always in the cards. Be sensitive to the possibility that your closest supporters may need time to adjust to their own feelings before being able to offer encouragement and support to you.

As you think about questions to ask these trusted souls, first ask yourself:

- What is the most valuable support I receive from this individual? Encouragement? Analysis? Direction? Listening? Perspective? Data?

- What am I looking for from him/her in the way of support *at this moment* in relation to my decision?

- Is that something this individual can truly offer right now? Does their toolbox of solutions fit this situation? Do they speak the language of this journey? Are they flexible enough to look with fresh eyes at my situation?

- Does my choice raise questions about their own career or the quality of their life going forward, or the effect on other family members? If so, address these tangential discussions separately.

Many resources are available to help you make the best decisions for you. Besides resources described earlier, there are innumerable internet-based career resources as well as local workshops and career coaches. Four great resources often overlooked include:

*Your alma mater.* If you have higher education or certificate credentials under your belt, contact the institution's career service office or job board coordinator. If you know what field you intend to pursue, these experts may be able to get you in touch with other alums working in that area. If you are undecided about the next avenue to pursue, these pros may have examples of others who have switched from your first career to something else. Unless swamped by the demands of current students, they are typically motivated to speak with you. Besides your charming personality or altruistic reasons, simply put, when you do well they look good. Plus, alums are a major source of funding for most higher education institutions. When you are happily employed and they helped, they are hoping you will remember.

*The alumni organization.* This can be the alumni organization of a school you attended or the alumni organization of a school you wish to attend. The group might meet in person, online through the school, or connect via social media such as LinkedIn or Facebook. These are individuals who share a common bond of campus stories, courses of study, professors, culture, and school philosophy. They have a framework in which to envision you as a learner and a professional. Some of the best networking before and after school can come through alumni groups.

*Professional associations.* Many career fields can be explored through national professional associations. These groups are likely to have current data on what it takes to break into the field, the outlook for jobs in the near future, and networking programs where you can meet with individuals in the field. The design and presentation of material on the website can provide insight into the personality of the field, as well as details about the work. If you are a student, check out student rates for workshops and conferences where you can be immersed in the culture and discuss hot topics with professionals in this field.

*Educational institution websites.* Click on all the links. Each site reflects the character of the institution in some way. In addition, if you hope to transition to a new field without retraining, course descriptions will let you know what the new-graduate competition will be bringing to the table. These descriptions may even provide key terms or phrases that accurately reflect your experience but aren't on your resume—yet.

## Legacy

Almost twenty years ago an historian friend and I sat contemplating what positive legacy our generation could possibly leave for our children. Both of us had grown weary by the relentless change that disrupted our hopes for stability. Change with no end in sight appeared to be our future. We reflected on the extraordinary legacies of those that had gone before us; legacies that led to civil rights breakthroughs, put a man on the moon, created the internet, and made heart transplants possible. Our own accomplishments were possible only because we "stood on the shoulders of [those] giants" (Alice Walker). We had been given so much. What valuable lessons could our lives marked by constant change possibly offer the next generation?

In a moment of comic relief, it struck us. A well-known dorm poster in our youth declared, "When life gives you lemons, make lemonade!" If change was our lemon, surviving and thriving through change was to be our legacy (or lemonade, if you will.) How to embrace change, understand change, evaluate change, approach change, seek change, appreciate change and move forward with change. Our generation could provide a blueprint for wholeheartedly pursuing a goal and then shifting gears with ease when "life" happens.

Through our own ups and downs, my friend and I would seek to become the Zen masters of change, befriending and existing with change rather than attempting to control or eliminate it. We would embrace lifelong learning, take calculated risks, and turn failures into opportunities for renewal and surprise. Most importantly, we would learn how to let go of expired expectations and move forward.

From that day forward each change we faced was an opportunity, another chance to write the new story. Through challenges, set-backs, and successes, we continue to cheer each other on, keeping the long- term vision of legacy in our mind's eye. But far more important than individual triumphs is the image that even in chaos and unpredictable change it is possible to identify a target, a goal, a

16

purpose, a dream—and go for it. That is our legacy. As you consider the next steps in your life, what will be your legacy?

## SUMMARY

In Chapter One we explored topics and questions that have led many adults back to the classroom. Shifts in societal expectations and personal opportunities have opened new doors. Unrelenting change requires constant reinvention. The desire to leave something positive for the next generation calls for meaningful work with a purpose that matters. Often, this means going back to school.

Chapter One confirmed that you are not alone. Far from it. Adults are returning to school in record numbers. In a June 2008 report, *Reach Higher, America*, the National Commission on Adult Literacy recommended that state and federal governments prepare to accommodate twenty million adult learners annually by 2020. The Commission further recommended that Congress pass a new act to "excite the public imagination" and likened the project to historical achievements such as the original GI Bill of 1944 and the National Interstate and Defense Highways Act of 1956. One year later in his 2009 American Graduation Initiative, President Barack Obama set a new goal for America to have the highest proportion of college graduates in the world by 2020. America is going back to school.

Your next step is to walk one-by-one through the questions that stand between you and a go/no-go decision to return to school. Make your list of questions. Then move on to Chapter Two where we tackle six pressing questions rarely discussed in educational marketing materials but often raised by those contemplating this journey:

- Is this the best time?

- Am I too old?

- Where do I fit?

- Am I capable?

- What does it take to become a ___?

- Is it worth it?

17

# CHAPTER TWO

# A JOURNEY CONSIDERED

"The minute you start,
there is a light at the end of the tunnel."

Experienced travelers develop practices to decide when, where, and how to travel. As each new journey is considered, maps appear, guidebooks are purchased, and casual conversation turns to discussion of the potential destination. Questions are answered. Unknowns are clarified. Risks are mitigated. All are weighed against the traveler's goal, purpose, and timeline. Each step in the process increases and refines the information essential for a good travel experience. At some point, data collection and analysis stop. A decision is made with full understanding that there will be surprises and changes along the way. The traveler is ready.

Returning to school is a significant journey. Unfortunately there are no maps and few guidebooks for this trip—a deficit this book begins to fill. As with our traveler, many concerns can be mitigated by asking a few basic questions. "Is this the best time to go?" "How much will it cost?" "What must I bring along to succeed?" "What are the people like?" "What will be expected of me?" "And even, do I need vaccinations or special medical insurance?"

This chapter guides the reader through six questions that provide an initial framework for the back-to-school decision. Consider each question. Then think like our traveler; recognize when you have enough information for now and move on. There will be ample opportunity to revisit each question along the way.

## Is This the Best Time?

That depends. Much has been written about travel to Paris in the springtime, but does that mean spring is the best time for everyone to travel? Absolutely not. The best time for you to return to school depends on a combination of factors specific to you. Examples include your educational and career goals, current family and job responsibilities, personal health, available funding, and your personal support system. Economic conditions such as job obsolescence or layoff may prompt or accelerate a decision to return to school. Or perhaps a number of events have come together and it simply feels like the time is right. If you are wondering if this is the best time to return to school, ask yourself the following questions:

- *Do I have a choice?* Has your first career gone the way of buggy whip manufacturing? Was it eliminated by obsolescence, outsourcing, or changes in the economy? If so, then your time to return to school is now.

- *Is my current field of work in jeopardy?* If predictions for the survival of your current field are dire, don't waste time holding on to a sinking ship. When time is of the essence, take steps to explore your interests and options. The sooner you start, the more likely you will minimize or eliminate a period of unemployment.

- *Am I strongly motivated to return to school right now?* If it just feels like the right time to get that degree, go for it. If you are compelled toward a specific type of work but want to make sure there are likely to be jobs upon graduation, ask professionals in that field about the timing. Is there a shortage? Are workers being laid off or jobs outsourced? Are

20

positions of interest to you being advertised? What do the pundits say about long-term viability of this field? Take it all in then make your own decision.

- *What personal considerations are in the mix?* Do you need to maintain an income while you go to school? If your current position is relatively stable, can you continue to work while taking classes? Does your current employer offer tuition reimbursement? What family facts and dynamics must be considered? Are you physically, mentally, and financially fit for the journey or do you need time to get in shape?

## AM I TOO OLD?

This question deserves special attention as it looms larger with each passing day. First, if you believe you are too old and there is no chance to change your point of view, you are indeed too old. Attitude plays a significant role in the correct answer to this question.

Second, there are a few occupations that do have age limitations based on practicality or rules. Find out if the career of your dreams falls into this category. Three examples are professional orchestra musicians, commercial pilots, and physicians. Ask any full-time orchestra member when he/she first took up his/her instrument and you are likely to get a single-digit answer. No matter how youthful you may feel, if you are reading this book it is probably too late to realistically become a paid member of the Philadelphia Orchestra—although it is never too late to learn to play for humanity.

Likewise, some commercial airlines have a mandatory retirement age around sixty for pilots. Thus, if you are over fifty it is unlikely you will have time to train and gain the requisite expertise to be considered hirable. You can still become a pilot, but probably not captain for a major commercial carrier on international flights. Similarly, medical schools tend to shy away from applicants older than forty simply because of the years needed to gain proficiency as a physician. These are not hard facts but something to consider.

Third, and this is very important, there is a big gap between being *capable* of becoming proficient in a field and being *accepted* as a candidate for hire into that field. Very smart people often confuse the two. If you have the financial freedom to pursue your dreams with no concern about financial payback, go for it. If not, take time to explore acceptance levels for nontraditional-age entrants before running up a student loan debt.

Getting to the truth may take some digging, particularly given the undertones of ageism in truthful responses. Do not assume you will be one of the rare exceptions—no matter what your job history suggests. Find out what life is like for the average second-career graduate in your target position. If this is not acceptable for your overall life plans, don't give up, but like a careful traveler who weighs available data before leaving home, make a note for later reflection.

Many people need answers that are more concrete. For readers who do, the following AITO formula (Am I Too Old?) was created just for you. The AITO formula is an age-based indicator. Other considerations such as the wisdom of taking on student loan debt are dealt with later in this book.

## THE AITO (AM I TOO OLD?) FORMULA

| | |
|---|---|
| 1. How old are you? | _____ |
| 2. How long do you need in the next career (in order to earn $X income, save for retirement, gain benefits?) | _____ |
| 3. Add the number of years it may take for training and getting up to speed as a professional. | _____ |
| 4. Add the length of time a go/no-go decision is likely to take. | _____ |
| Total: | = _____ |

If this number is equal to or less than the age at which you envision not working (or shifting to part-time or volunteer work), you are good to go. If the answer is higher than that age, ask yourself if you can reduce any of the numbers in the calculation? Are there faster ways to gain the necessary training or credentials through night and summer courses, internships, or part-time employment? If not, does working abroad appeal to you? According to friends who have established international teaching and consulting careers, the expertise of older workers is revered and sought out in cultures such as Asia, Latin America, and Africa.

Be realistic and thorough in deciding the length of time required to reach a go/no-go decision. What is the timeframe for applications? Are you in the middle of an all-consuming project? Many advanced degree programs require infrequently-offered entrance exams, start new classes only in the fall, and have specific deadlines for applications and financial aid consideration. Sketching out a time line may help you identify a realist answer for number four in the AITO formula.

If your answer to number four is still a problem for you, consider if the real question is not whether this is a good time or if you are too old, but rather, "Do I really want to?" If this rings true for you, take a moment to reflect on what you really want and what you need to get there. This is *your* life—make sure this is *your* decision. A major derailer for returning students is trying to fulfill someone else's educational dream; one that the student doesn't embrace.

If you feel motivated but decision making is a personal challenge, apply techniques that led to past achievement of goals. Address personality tendencies toward procrastination before diving into advanced education. Drawing a timeline may be helpful if you are a visual learner. And remember, it is OK to ask for help all along the way!

## AITO Example

Bill is a teacher thinking about becoming an education law attorney. Bill hopes to retire by age 65. His retirement funds and working spouse make it possible for him to consider next-career options in a ten-year period. He estimates he'll need three years for law school and another three years to build know-how and reputation as an attorney. Although Bill's take-charge personality could comfortably make a go/no-go decision in under two minutes, Bill realizes there is more to consider.

It is January 28 and Bill is swamped with his teaching assignment. It is clear he won't have time to study for the entrance exams until summer. Because the exams are only offered a few times each year, he decides to register for the fall test, get his score and then work on applications during fall break. Bill knows from speaking with admission representatives that acceptance letters are typically sent in the spring—which in Bill's schedule is more than a year from today. Once he learns the details of acceptance, nonacceptance, financial aid, and so forth, he will be able to decide. Doing the math, it appears that it could take up to eighteen months before a final decision about attending law school will be possible for Bill. Here is Bill's AITO score:

## BILL's AITO DATA

| | | |
|---|---|---|
| 1. | How old are you? | 45 |
| 2. | How long a career-run do you need in the next career (in order to earn $X income, gather savings, qualify for retirement, or receive other benefits?) | 10 |
| 3. | Add the number of years it may take for training and getting up to speed as a professional. | 6 |
| 4. | Add the length of time a go/no-go decision is likely to take. | 1.5 |
| | Total: | = 62.5 |

Since Bill had hopes to no longer be engaged in full-time employment by age sixty-five, Bill wins on the AITO score! Again, this does not take into account the wisdom of Bill selling his home, abandoning his family, and living in a trailer down by the river for several years to pay for law school (or amassing debt comparable to the gross national product of a small country). Neither does this AITO score say anything about the availability of attorney jobs down the road or Bill's chances of being hired. At this point, we are simply considering if sufficient time exists in relationship to Bill's age.

Now it is your turn. Here are sample questions to get you started.

- What is your AITO score for the career you are considering?

- If the numbers suggest there is not enough time to meet your next career goals, what can be done to reduce the time to fully transition to the next career?

- What is your greatest concern about the time it will take to make a decision? Take one step today to reduce that concern.

Whatever your answers are to the preceding questions, there is one final thought to remember: *time marches on no matter what*. If a three-year (or one year or six year) degree seems like a long time, you can either be three years older WITH the new degree or WITHOUT the new degree. Either way, you will be three years older.

## WHERE DO I FIT?

A good career fit, like a good pair of hiking shoes, is measured by whether or not this choice will take you where you want to go (and ideally in the condition you want to be in at the end of the journey). The best-made hiking boots on earth do no good at all if they are a poor fit. Likewise, the best career for your brother-in-law could be your worst nightmare.

Today career options include thousands of jobs that didn't exist when many of us took our first position—online instructor, iPod designer, coffee barista, pet psychologist, and nanotechnologist to name a few. How do you decide where you'll fit when the jobs available at graduation don't exist when you choose a major?

Imagine you were just granted a six-week, all-expense-paid, first-class trip to travel anywhere in the world. How would you decide where to go? A past favorite spot? A destination on your "someday" list? A suggestion from a travel magazine or AAA brochure? A place you have read about, heard of from friends, or seen in a film or on TV?

Identifying a new career is much the same. Start with careers that *sparked* your interest when encountered in your daily activities. If you are easily sparked, consider this a Top Ten list. Ideally, there will be five or fewer careers. These can be held by friends or relatives, professionals you have worked with or hired, careers of those who have helped you or a family member, careers you have seen in volunteer organizations, careers in the news, in books, on the web, TV, or film. Now, step back and look for recurring themes. Do these jobs all require working with children? With people in need? Technology? Travel? This is your starting point for further exploration.

For example, when I was looking at master's degree programs I attended a six-week career exploration course where, among other things, we identified jobs we thought we would like to do. My list included midwife, corporate information specialist, orchestra manager, and attorney. As odd as these may appear, the underlying theme was working with people to help them get from where they were to where they wanted to be. The best fit for me at that point in my life emerged as I explored the details of each field and related options. The outcome was a master's degree in industrial relations that led to a fifteen-year professional career.

Good occupational fit is measured at a given point in time by a mix of factors important to the workplace and to you. What is important to you today? Time? Title? Flexibility? Training? Calmness or excitement? Growth opportunities? The perfect accountant at a large, stable company might be an awful fit in a razzle-dazzle start-up environment. Likewise, positions that require extensive travel or long hours may be a great fit for you at some point but not so good when you have personal or family commitments. In my situation, this analysis knocked midwife and attorney right off my list. Too many years of training with four young children at home.

"But will I *like* being a dog groomer (or astrophysicist)?" you ask. Nothing answers that question like real life experience. Look for opportunities to volunteer in your area of interest. Even a one-time project can connect you to professionals in the field and provide insight about the work. If you'd like a bit more, check out Vocation Vacations, an innovative company that offers the opportunity to spend a few days working alongside a professional in your field of interest. Currently more than 100 mentors are available around the country to explore professions from wine maker to alpaca farmer to TV script writer. Had this been around ten years ago you can bet I'd have been all over this one.

For those on a more restricted budget, conduct a Google search on your topic area or browse the relevant section of your local library or book store. Once you locate relevant information, do a self-check. If you are impatient or feel a desire to flee, take note. If, on the other hand, you are immersed in the topic and have lost track of time, also take note. Although not scientifically proven as a measurement of occupational fit, rethink spending years of education in a field in which ten minutes of library research feels like a lifetime.

If the course of study you are considering requires an entrance exam, check out relevant study guides. Entrance tests are designed to assess whether you have what it takes to succeed in a given area of study. Although research indicates these exams are fair and accurate predictors of success, take your score with a grain of salt. Test-taking is its own skill. If you loved the questions but scored poorly, don't eliminate this field unless additional data suggests it isn't a good match. On the other hand, if the questions are interesting to you and are easy for you to answer, that may be a good sign.

Assessments are another readily available tool to hone in on areas of potential fit. Consider taking a vocational interest assessment and a personality assessment. The most well-known vocational interest assessment is the Strong Interest Inventory (SII) (formerly the Strong-Campbell Interest Inventory) and its contemporary cousin the CISS® (Campbell™ Interest and Skill Survey). If you took a test in high school that said you should be a flight attendant, minister, or fire fighter, it was probably the Strong-Campbell. Teams of experts have identified common interest sets among successful professionals in a number of specific fields. If the assessment matches you with flight attendants, your likes and dislikes (as identified by you in the assessment) are similar to interests selected by actual flight attendants. Theoretically, this implies you, too, would enjoy working as a flight attendant. On the other hand, it may just mean you'd like to hang out with them.

Two of the most widely respected personality assessments are the Myers-Briggs Type Indicator and the DiscProfile. Both instruments look at personal preferences in relation to behavioral choices and environment. Each is frequently used in career development and corporate team building programs. Viewed side by side, the results of your vocational and personality assessments provide insight to possible career interests as well as careers from which to run like the dickens. Compare your assessment results to the top five careers that sparked your interest in the earlier paragraph. Circle careers that appear in more than one of your lists. If there is no overlap, that's fine, too. Perhaps there are subtle similarities. Do many of the identified occupations deal with people in one-to-one situations? Require working with numbers and data? Are hands-on jobs? Strategic jobs? Look closely enough and you are likely to find a useful theme.

To get the maximum benefit, take each assessment as part of a workshop or locate a psychologist to administer the instrument and interpret your results. High quality assessments are only available through professionals with advanced degrees or a specialized certification to interpret the results. If money is tight, look for opportunities to take one of these instruments through community education, alumni career service offices, or church-based job support groups.

The downside of vocational and personality assessments is that these tools tell you zip about your ability to actually *be* a flight attendant. The theory suggests you might enjoy a certain activity, but it says nothing of your requisite skill to make a profession of it. Still, these instruments can uncover hidden motivations or highlight a career field not previously considered.

A good example is the story of a young woman whose career as a dancer was cut short by knee injuries. The Strong Campbell pointed her to occupational therapy, a field she knew nothing about. Quick research indicated that OTs methodically and creatively assist injured individuals to reclaim the tasks of daily living—much like her real life as a dancer. Last year she was honored by her peers at the nationally recognized rehabilitation center where she now works.

Once you have narrowed your list to five or fewer career fields, dig in to learn the current realities of each area of interest. Every career has its own quirks and culture. Again, nothing is better than experience. Check out Vocation Vacations or create your own shadow opportunity. Meet with practitioners to get a real world view of the field. Be respectful, but ask direct questions to get at the heart of what "fit" means for you.

Sometimes what appears at first to be a great fit in terms of skill and personality doesn't fit at all with current realities of the job. For example, as trends indicated medicine was losing brilliant, caring, science-oriented young people to other pursuits, research revealed an increasing lack of "fit" with the image of working around the clock, being tied to a pager, and simultaneously managing an office. The fit as doctor was different from the fit as doctor + business administrator + round-the-clock-employee. In response, medical students now have the option to specialize as a hospitalist, a physician whose primary focus is the care of hospitalized patients. Unlike traditional clinic positions, a hospitalist physician has predictable work weeks and hours and minimal administrative work. The hospitalist role provides a valuable new option for the next generation of doctors.

A few points follow that provide additional insight about fit.

- *Culture.* Describe the settings in which you are most comfortable. Describe individuals who are comfortable with you.

- *Interests.* What type of work energizes you? If all financial needs were taken care of, what would you do for free?

- *Personality.* What field of professionals do you feel at home with? Imagine you are in the middle seat on a twelve-hour flight? Describe the personalities of the individuals you would most want to be seated on either side of you. What if it were a two-hour flight?

- *Values.* In the last year, where have you spent your time and money? What were the three most difficult choices? What value influenced each choice?

## AM I CAPABLE?

No matter how long it has been since you were in school, chances are you have the necessary smarts to succeed. The bigger question is whether you have "what it takes" to do so. A Grand Canyon-size difference exists between personal talent and the stuff it takes to apply that talent. Some average individuals attain significant achievements while others with tremendous talent languish in both work and personal life, seemingly unable to connect talent and action.

There are two phases to a successful return to school. Phase one includes everything it takes to get to the first day of class, from the decision to pursue a specific program to the day you buy your books. Phase two begins when you take your seat (or log in) for your first class and ends when you walk across the stage to receive your diploma. Phase one requires intention demonstrated by action, personal motivation to achieve, and the ability to be true to oneself. Phase two requires all three of these and a bit more (to be described in Chapter Three). First, let's take a closer look at phase one.

**Intention and Action**

Many people contemplate returning to school. Fewer actually get there. Phase one of "what it takes" separates the talkers from the doers. The first step is intention.

Intention is an internal psychological state that consciously and subconsciously influences our attitudes and goals. Intentions guide action. Actions are the external manifestation of intention. To understand someone's intentions, look closely at their actions.

Intention with no action is a mere daydream. Action with no intention is random. Intention and action run along a continuum marked by increasing levels of intensity. High levels of intention frequently correlate with high levels of action although there is no guarantee. Think about the following career- and education-related scenarios. Where do you fall on each continuum?

### *Intention Continuum*
### No intention→Some intention→Strong intention

*No intention.* Your conversations about returning to school or changing careers are random and perfunctory, something to talk about in a social setting besides the weather, sports, or politics. Ideas and opinions exchanged during the conversations do not continue in your head when you drive home. You are rarely, if ever, lost in thought about what you might want to do next in your career life.

*Some intention.* You may have initiated a conversation or two. When thoughts of going back to school enter your mind, you ponder them with minimal attention and passing interest. If an old friend calls and asks what's new, you may or may not mention thoughts of returning to school. If asked directly if you are considering going back to school, your typical response is, "I'm thinking about it."

*Strong intention.* You have probably read several books and spent significant time researching educational programs and career change on the web. It is likely you have initiated informational interviews (formal and informal), attended job groups, and paid for workshops or coaching. You may have even attended career fairs or college information sessions. Friends and family know you are considering educational options. You frequently think about the possibilities and how to make it all work. (Notice how much action appears at this level of intention.)

### *Action Continuum*
### No action→Some action→Strong action

*No action.* [College catalogs or career books in your possession were purchased by someone else.]

*Some action.* You might pick up a book or two about returning to school or changing careers, although you are more likely to ask someone else about their resources rather than do research on your own. You arrange to speak with someone you know about her career. Your calendar averages at most one activity a week related to going back to school or new careers.

*Strong action.* You check out recommended resources. You research the possibility of returning to school as if it were a part-time job (or as close as is possible). You network through various avenues (friends, social networking sites, professional organizations) to find professionals with whom to speak. You prepare questions for informational interviews and send thank you notes afterwards. You apply to educational programs. You synthesize the information you collect, analyze it, and decide how it does or does not apply to your next step. Your calendar reflects several activities per week related to school and careers.

Those who appear to be all talk and no action often have very different intentions than their words suggest. This confuses those closest to them because it sounds like the individual is planning to do something, whereas in reality, the individual's intentions are nowhere near action (as evidenced by the lack thereof). In some instances, true intention is achieved by the act of talking, period. The individual may simply be talking to deflect someone who thinks he *should* go back to school or change careers. He may just want to participate in the current conversation. Or, his personality may be one that processes information and ideas out loud. In those situations, talking is the action that achieves the goal, or true intention. No further action is needed.

Whatever the case, if you find you are doing a lot of talking but lacking action, step back and ask yourself, "What truly are *my* interests, goals, and intentions?" If a close look reveals that your true intention is to keep well-meaning others at bay, give yourself permission to stop the charade, embrace the you that you want to be, and tell them thanks, but no thanks. You'll be doing each of you a favor.

If your true intention is to return to school to establish a new career, ask yourself, "What is getting in the way of action?" Are you overwhelmed or confused about where to begin? Are you concerned about the potential effect on family or friends? Has life been too busy—really (not as an excuse)? As you continue reading through this book, earmark pages that offer helpful-sounding tips for you— then connect intention with action and try them!

## Achievement Motivation

Intention and action will get you a long way toward return-ing to school but there is more. Rita's friends don't get it. For years, Rita has talked about returning to school. She collects brochures, attends information sessions, even completed an application. But here she is, still talking. No one is pushing her; this is clearly her idea. But when she gets close to submitting her application, some-thing always comes up that takes precedence. The time never seems right—and that's OK with Rita. Either it will happen someday or it won't. Rita would like to achieve her goal but won't feel like she truly missed out if she doesn't.

Kristina and Victor are a study in contrast to Rita. Step by step Kristina selected a program, completed the prerequisites, studied and took the entrance exam, carefully prepared her application, and is awaiting an acceptance decision for the fall term. And yes, she has a back-up plan. Two months ago, Victor's boss suggested he had a lot of potential and should consider completing his degree. Within days Victor set his sights on a specific program and fast-tracked the details to make it happen as soon as possible. Kristina and Victor have different personalities but both have their sights set on getting the degree. Rita is motivated, but Kristina and Victor have something more. They possess a specific type of motivation called achievement motivation.

Breaking from traditional theory at the time, Harvard psychologist David McClelland (1917-1998) viewed success as a measure of this personal trait which he labeled achievement motivation. McClelland theorized that the "need to achieve" is motivation that varies between individuals and can be measured. Rita will still be happy if she never quite makes it back to school. Kristina and Victor haven't considered that option.

This may sound like a blinding flash of the obvious, but here is the rub. According to McClelland, individuals with a *high* need for achievement tend to not be big risk takers. Instead, they seek moderately difficult but reachable challenges. They balance their need to achieve with the likelihood of success. They are willing to work hard but must believe it is possible to get the A. Failure is not a comfortable option.

Those with *low* needs for achievement seek either 1) very easy tasks with guaranteed success (and little sense of achievement) or 2) highly difficult tasks perceived to be out of reach (making potential failure not embarrassing thus creating a low personal risk). In the first case, personal potential is sacrificed in order to take the easiest available route to a guaranteed goal. Alternatively, the individual may sign up for classes that intimidate others but look like fun to him or her. Armed with an it-doesn't-hurt-to-try attitude, failure isn't a showstopper. Skills and abilities are applied step by step, milestone by milestone, until the individual has gone as far as he or she cares to go. A low need for achievement can be a roadblock to goal achievement or a springboard to opportunity. Taylor epitomizes the latter. She has a low need to achieve but a curiosity to try "interesting" things. Taylor leads a varied and highly successful career life in large part because she doesn't fear failure as most of us define it. "What's the worst that can happen?" she says with an unruffled smile. "Maybe I'll need to learn something new or ask for help. No problem. And if they fire me, I'll try something else."

Back to our friends Rita, Kristina, and Victor. Given her low need to achieve, if Rita returns to school she may select an easy program that minimally meets her goal and won't disrupt the more important activities of her daily life. Or, Rita may truly shock her friends and decide to go after a challenging major just because she thinks it might be fun. The lesson for Rita is to make sure she selects a program she'll feel was worthwhile five years from now, rather than one that is merely a cinch to pass. Otherwise she could end up spending the same amount of time and money as if she had gone to a more rigorous program, but walk away with a lot less.

Kristina and Victor have a different challenge. In their drive to return to school, they may skip over choices that are a better match for their long-term goals but have a more challenging admissions process. I see this often with students who want to earn a master's in business administration degree (MBA) but only consider programs that don't require typical entrance exams (typically the Graduate Record Exam or Graduate Management Admissions Test). Fear of tests or specifically, math, isn't worth the risk of rejection. Whereas Rita would likely shrug off poor test scores or rejection and move on, Kristina and Victor nervously await the results; and are troubled when the score falls shy of their target.

While both Kristina and Victor are more likely than Rita to attain their educational goals, they are less likely to choose a program that could maximize their potential. Instead, Kristina and Victor may opt for programs that are moderately difficult but where they are likely to be at the top of the class. This is a fine thing, and may be their best choice. However, the lesson for these two is to make sure not to sacrifice a lifelong dream in order to remain in one's comfort zone. So you take the statistics class three times. Who cares as long as you get where you want to go?

Whatever level of achievement motivation you possess, you can successfully return to school. Just make sure to ask yourself if the program you've selected is the one you'll most likely be happy with down the road. The immediate answer isn't nearly as important as taking time to consider the question.

## Remaining True to Oneself

Friends and family are great observers of our abilities and weaknesses. They can provide insight into our talents and encouragement to face a challenge. They can also unintentionally point us in the wrong direction.

Has a friend or relative said to you, "You are so good at _____. You would make a great _____!" Unless this individual is a hiring manager with open positions, take this advice with a grain of salt. Often one's image of what it takes to succeed in a field is very, very different from the real deal. If, however, you hear the same suggestion from several people, consider it, but do your own research.

Likewise, this same well-meaning friend may be unaware of talents you *want* to use in a next career. Returning to school is a time to pursue talents that were left behind or have not been explored—or ditch talents that brought success but not personal fulfillment in a first career. This is your time. Embrace it.

Kelli, a human resource executive, had a reputation for engineering the "kinder, gentler layoff," but hated every minute of these experiences. When Kelli went to law school, she intentionally avoided employment law. Instead, she chose to apply her collaborative problem solving and strategic thinking talents in new practice areas. Kelli's friends and family couldn't understand why she would let go of years of experience rather than use her professional background as a foundation for her law career. Although well-intentioned, they did not know about the dreams Kelli gave up many years back; nor did they truly understand how she felt about her work life in this field.

Friends and family often base their beliefs on what they have seen; in other words, the work you have done up to now. Like Kelli, only you know what these facts are for you. Before seeking opinions about your ability to pursue a new direction, ask yourself these questions.

- Among your friends and family, who do you most trust to accurately assess your abilities and interests? Why this person?

- Is this still true regarding a back-to-school decision? If not, who would it be and why?

Next time someone suggests what you "should" be or do, thank them for their support and interest, check their idea against your list, and see if it sticks.

## What Does it Take to Become a ...?

You've decided it is as good a time as any to go back to school. You are a picture of youth and you have at least a gut feel for the potential career fit. Friends and family are behind you. You are motivated and your intentions are evident through action. Now you need to find out if you have (or can acquire) what it takes to break into this field.

Here is where networking and informational interviewing skills get put to work! The best way to determine how to get somewhere is to ask someone who was there recently enough to know the current path. Talk to professors whose students enter this field. Find out what new grads are expected to know. Talk to people who work in your area of interest. Learn what it takes to succeed. Ask questions about educational and/or certification requirements for jobs. Get their insights and recommendations about academic programs, what the life of a successful professional in their field looks like, and what it takes long term to succeed in their field.

Below are some networking and informational interview questions to get you started:

- What led you to go into this field?

- What skill or ability has been the most important for your success in this career?

- What has changed since you began?

- What do you get paid to do?

- What are the opportunities or unmet needs in this field? (Focus on their industry or the field in general or it may sound like a trick request for employment.)

- What one thing did you wish you had known when you chose this field?

- What was the best thing you did during your schooling?

- What would you do differently?

If you are stumped about the path one might take to enter a specific line of work, go to any state university website. Search related key words under sections headed "academics," "courses," or "majors and minors." For example, if you want to learn how to become an actuary search the terms actuary, business, math, and statistics.

Take note of the path you choose as you explore this site. Did something besides actuary pique your curiosity? Did the website make you want to run away screaming? Pay attention to what grabs your attention. Limit the amount of time you spend. Get in and get out. If that isn't possible but the concept sounds like a good idea, pick up (or order) a paper version of the college catalog. A few colleges still have them.

## Is It Worth It?

And now for the $50,000 question (or $125,000 question if you are considering law school). Is it worth it? Is the cost worth the benefit?

These four little words demand a yes or no answer. Yet reaching the conclusion requires synthesis of collected data, personal wisdom, and yet-unknown (and perhaps unknowable) facts. To ask "Is it worth it?" is to inquire about personal risk and sacrifice; to seek confirmation that the benefit of the outcome will meet or exceed the cost of the journey; to reach a clear go/no-go decision.

Precedence for analysis of this question is found in a well-known legal proceeding where the defendant responded by simply stating, "It depends on what the meaning of the word 'is' is." In our case it depends on one's interpretation of "it," "worth," and the second "it." Or put another way, does the cost justify the outcome?

### The First "It:" Cost and Risk

Is what worth it? The time, effort, expense? Foregone income, rebuilding a network, altering a lifestyle temporarily or permanently? The first "it" seeks to measure personal and financial cost and risk. It inquires how returning to school might impact the way one lives life, right now, with friends and family.

For example, time and effort spent on re-education is time and energy that becomes unavailable to friends and family. Reduction in income or debt incurred to pay for school may alter spending patterns. Costs may include the risk that friends will part ways. Family may be asked to make sacrifices in support of your goals. If things don't work out as planned after graduation, what will you have given up to get there?

Determining the details of the first "it" is an intensely personal question, one only you and your gut can answer.

## Worth: The Value Proposition

Next we turn to the central term of our question: worth. Worth is a hard concept to pin down. Definitions range from the tangible ("This vase is worth $12.") to the ambiguous ("He ran for all he was worth."). Although laden with multiple interpretations, worth in our context is the monetary and personal value associated with educational pursuit.

Monetary value, like market worth, determines if the price tag is about right, too high, or a great deal. Personal value determines if you care. Just because lutefisk is on sale at the supermarket doesn't mean everyone will rush to fill their freezers. On the other hand, people stand in line to pay $6 for a foot long corn dog at the State Fair because, well, it wouldn't be the State Fair without a corn dog. In the latter case, personal value includes ambiance and tradition for which the buyers are willing to pay. In the lutefisk example, the cost savings is irrelevant because, well, many people would pay to NOT eat it.

Like the center of an Oreo, worth is the filling in the middle—squished between costs and risks on one side and benefits, expectations, and hopes on the other. And as many Oreo lovers would concur, the middle is the essence of the whole. Without a clear picture of something's value *to us*, we don't know if $50 for a lamp is a bargain or a rip-off.

Let's look at an example of worth determination. It is twenty degrees below zero outside. There are blizzard warnings. You were planning to go to a concert but now you're wondering, "is it worth it?" How do you decide the value or "worth" of the concert? You might weigh factors that are important to you at the time (this might really be Cher's last concert), recall past experience (snowdrifts aren't that much fun to navigate), or the wisdom (or demands) of important others. Perhaps the tickets were purchased months in advance, expensive, or the artist is way cool. Maybe the concert is the central reunion activity of high school buddies counting on your attendance (or maybe you never liked these people anyway and the snow is a great excuse). Perhaps the concert required no tickets for fancy seats but features the Lincoln Elementary first grade class, including your child (or for some of us...grandchild); and, to increase the stakes, you are the child's transportation.

As you look at your snow-covered vehicle, the wind squealing as it whips through the bare trees, mental images of camaraderie or pride (personal value) are carefully weighed against lost ticket money (monetary value.)

Next you weigh the cost and risk to go to the event or to not go against the expected benefits; back and forth, back and forth like an endless tennis match in your mind. Eventually an overall sense of worth is determined for this activity within the current snowy context and the mental game of pros and cons declares a winner.

To determine worth as it pertains to going back to school, start by considering the following provocative questions. These questions are independent in nature; a "no" to one question does not imply a hard stop in your journey.

- Is the vision of returning to school appealing?

- Does returning to school have substantial *personal* value to you? Is a degree something you've always wanted? Imagine yourself at ninety years of age with and without the certificate or degree. How do you feel?

- Does your vision of the next career reflect a compelling image of contribution to the world or to a specific purpose?

- What might the end look like if you were to "run for all you are worth" toward this goal? Describe two or three scenarios in which you did precisely that. How does the image of returning to school compare?

As with the first "it," only you can truly determine the value or worth of pursuing further education at this time in your life. The accurate answer for you combines facts with hope, all measured through your perception of the way things are today and the way they might be tomorrow.

## The Second "It:" Benefits and Outcomes

Now to address the second "it," the last term in our question, "Is it worth it?" To return to an earlier metaphor, if the first side of the Oreo dealt with cost and risk, and the middle inquired about the ultimate value to you, the flipside of the Oreo holds a personal image of one's hopes, dreams, assumptions, and expectations for such an endeavor—in other words, the personal benefit or outcome. The final "it" attempts to measure perceived benefit and outcome against reality.

This is a tall order for a very short word. What many people really want to know is if *given assumed cost, risk, and worth, is their vision for the next career* accurate enough *to justify the pursuit?* One's career vision might have tremendous personal and global worth with manageable cost and risk. Yet if the vision is an inaccurate reflection of reality, it is good to know before hopes are raised, money is spent, and time is forever lost.

The most accurate resources to determine the benefits or likely outcome of a particular course of education are:

- Those who are involved in this career right now (and ideally have at least three years tenure).

- Recent graduates with fewer than three years experience.

- A careful reading of timely professional articles, trustworthy trend predictions and job projections (including enrollment trends in related educational programs).

Perhaps most important is to clarify your personal definition of a desired benefit or outcome. If your primary goal is to earn a college degree, many paths will lead you there. If your primary goal is more specific such as to obtain a commercial pilot's license, work with horses and move to Greenland, you will need to consider educational options more carefully to ensure your desired outcome. A degree in art will give you a college degree but it might not be a direct line to a flying career involving horses in Greenland.

Remember, even if sacrifices loom large, the perceived value is sketchy and the benefit unclear, your only decision right now is whether or not to continue exploring the possibility of returning to school. If your decision involves lifelong dreams or goals, I encourage you to press on. Take the insights and unanswered questions from this chapter and keep reading.

## SUMMARY

Chapter One explored events that led to a world where returning to school is commonplace, and frequently essential. Chapter Two tackled questions of timing, age, fit, capability, and whether the outcome down the road might be worth the effort. The next step is to ask yourself some tough questions. Do I have what it takes to make it through? Is my area of interest a wise choice for me, personally and financially? How do you know what is reasonable to spend? This is the stuff of Chapter Three.

# Chapter Three

# It Really is All About You

"You are not who you were when you were last in school."

**W**elcome to the next chapter in your back-to-school journey! In this chapter we hear what adult students say it takes to succeed once you are in the classroom. Questions are posed to help confirm your choice of study area and direction. We tackle the topic of money, including the emotional side of funding your education. Charts and questions provide a framework to determine how much money is a reasonable amount to spend on your educational pursuits at this point in your life.

The final section of Chapter Three presents highlights from the Higher Education Professionals Survey designed and conducted exclusively for *Back to School for Grownups*. Professionals in higher education who work with adult students were asked to identify common characteristics of successful adult students and characteristics most likely to spell trouble. The chapter concludes with representative answers to the question, "What one thing should adult students returning to school know?"

# Ensuring Your Success

The decision to return to school is among life's biggest decisions—and biggest accomplishments. It can be very rewarding but requires planning and a lot of plain, old hard work. As an adult with a full plate of responsibilities, you already know something about hard work, planning, and accomplishments.

Think back to a favorite accomplishment. It doesn't matter if it happened yesterday or in sixth grade. It doesn't matter who knows what you did. There is insight to be gained from recalling the way you won the Scout badge, raised money for a good cause, overcame a personal fear, or transitioned to life in a new country. Each effort involved intention, action, motivation, creativity, and risk—and you did it.

## Making It Through

Big achievements require big effort. Look at Olympians and you'll start to see patterns of personalities. The same can be said for corporate executives or marathon runners, or parents, for that matter. Below are six characteristics frequently mentioned by successful adult students. Think about how they apply to you.

*Drive.* Definitions of drive imply moving something forward that doesn't go by itself. The successful student is one who will press on in the face of exhaustion, confusion, and way too much to do. If it were all fun and games there would be no need for graduation parties.

*Tenacity.* Tenacity or "stick-to-it-iveness" makes it possible to press on when the going gets tough. Tenacity fuels drive. Successful students stay with a task to completion. They ask questions to confirm understanding. If necessary, they retake the exam or the course. They keep going when others quit. Synonyms are courage, perseverance, and chutzpah.

*Network-savvy.* Students with good networking skills identify colleagues and faculty who can help them get through academic rough spots. They form study groups, ask questions, and find answers. In the process, these students develop relationships with classmates, professors, school administrators, and mentors who may help them get in front of potential employers—and perhaps obtain work in their field of study while still in school.

*Time-aware.* Successful students are aware of the passing of time. They may prefer to work ahead or wait until the last minute, knowing their best work is done under pressure. Either way, the point is that they know their own style and don't lose track of time. In contrast, students who lose track of time find themselves halfway through a three-hour exam with five minutes to go. Even if they know all the answers, they won't have the chance to demonstrate their knowledge. They get off-track running after tangential interests or some "bright shiny thing" of which there are many in school. Time-aware students look holistically at their commitments. They plan for the unexpected, leaving time for flexibility.

*Attention.* It has been said that the scarcest resource today is attention. No one knows this better than the adult student with a family and a full-time job. Yet time-pressed adults are some of the best students. These individuals employ a laser focused attention to the task at hand. They prioritize the activities vying for attention. They are mentally and physically present wherever they are. And they let go of each activity as they move on to the next.

## Staying Healthy

Another aspect of "you" that plays a significant role in academic success is personal health. An unforeseen health crisis (one's own or that of a family member) can throw a wrench into academic studies. So can failure to maintain good daily health habits. Eating a balanced diet, getting physical exercise, and taking time for quiet moments in the day serve as shock-absorbers for the added stress of studying. These practices also serve to balance school with the rest of life. Think small. This can be as simple as carrying water and healthy snacks to class, always parking at the far end of a parking lot, and taking a few extra minutes in the shower to relax tired muscles. Quality over quantity.

Equally important is one's mental health. School is exhilarating but also demanding. Make sure you give yourself mental breaks in your day. Sing in the car. Doodle in class. Choose a favorite picture or quote for your screensaver. Accept the fact that you won't be able to take all the classes or attend all the special activities you'd like. As odd as it sounds, follow the smokers outside on breaks simply to get the blood flowing and breathe fresh air.

Ironically, if ever there was a time for balance, this is it. If life is overwhelming, seek out someone with perspective who can help. A visit to the school counseling center or a trusted professor can make a world of difference. Take extra care if you are pursuing a program known for taxing students' emotional and physical well-being, such as medicine or law. In addition, many schools offer anonymous twelve-step programs for those concerned about substance abuse.

### Friends, Family, and School

Personal relationships can be extra challenging with one adult member in school. Loved ones may be our biggest supporters and demand little during school. However, even the best relationship may experience rough moments along the way. This topic deserves its own book, but given one short section, here are some thoughts.

First, talk with your friends and family before school starts. Be clear about your goals and what you hope to achieve through the academic program. Let them in on your vision and what it means to you. Share expectations (yours and theirs) about your availability during the first few weeks. Be conservative about the time you'll have available outside of work and school. Identify ways in which these individuals might help in the meantime (e.g., cooking meals, running errands, leaving you alone to study). Be appreciative up front and often.

Second, limit big social and family plans during the first semester. Give yourself space to figure out what you need. Find creative ways to include others. Some working couples set up a date night once a week (with the understanding that this might be cancelled during exam weeks). This assures the nonstudent that he/she is not forgotten while giving the student a framework around which to plan study time. Turn your required reading into bedtime stories for children (or grandchildren). Plan a social event to occur during semester break. Just about anything is tolerable when you know there is an end date.

Third, take time to thank your closest supporters all along the way. Appreciation in small but steady doses can be very powerful.

Use a family photo as a bookmark. Send a quick email of thanks to your significant other even though you will see him/her later in the day.

Find time each week to listen to the stories and concerns of those closest to you. Let them know they still matter. Put their gifts to use. "Study rocks" received as gifts from my grandsons during my school days still sit in clear view on my desk. The prominent display of the rocks reminded the boys that Grandma was thinking of them; and reminded me of more important things than grades.

## CONFIRMING YOUR CHOICE

Even after choosing an educational path to a new career, many returning adults wonder about the wisdom of their choice. Does it really make sense to tackle medical school at age fifty, or am I just nuts? If I take the time and money to retrain, will there be jobs at the end that will make the degree pay for itself or will I just be tired and broke? Will a master's degree in history lead to the next career of choice, or is it an expensive way to follow my passion?

The best answers for you depend on a mix of what you want out of the deal, as well as your personal characteristics, the economic realities of the time, and good fortune. For example, the decision to undertake the time and expense of medical school may indeed be wise for a medical technology scientist who retired early following a lucrative corporate acquisition and who hopes to provide free care to impoverished children. The same decision may not be as wise for someone of the same age with fewer financial resources or less medical background. Here is a three-step process you can use to ensure a wise educational choice.

*Step One.* Identify strengths and skills you can build on. A logical path between one career and the next means less work for you to get up to speed. It also connects the dots for college admissions staff and future hiring managers. If the link isn't crystal clear between where you've been and where you hope to go, be prepared to describe the link with confidence.

For example, Rick and Teri are thinking about second careers in pharmaceutical sales. Each has applied for admission to an MBA program. Rick is a successful community organizer for health care initiatives. Teri is an account clerk for the local school district. Details aside, stereotypes suggest our community organizer Rick may be more comfortable than account clerk Teri with the public speaking and assertive behavior required in the MBA program and a professional sales career. Teri can overcome this perception by painting a picture of herself as an assertive saleswoman in her admission essays, through her references, and by demonstrating her abilities during school through internships, volunteer activities, or other tangible means.

*Step Two.* Do your own investigation about your chosen field. It is possible to spend precious time and thousands of dollars gaining college credentials in fields that turn out to be a poor match, are overpopulated, or worse, rapidly becoming obsolete. This is important information that can ensure the wisdom of your choice. Even if the jobs for which you become certified are moved to India or entirely eliminated, your student loans are still due.

Look at the local, national, and international market for your field of interest, not because you might move to France, but because the global business environment means the available job may be with a company headquartered in France. Expand your research beyond web-based articles and college admissions staff. Talk to individuals new to the field, at mid-career, and near retirement. Each perspective will offer insight to the wisdom in pursuing this field as a next career. Prepare a list of five to eight thought-provoking (but not interviewee-provoking) questions. Here are some examples:

- What changes have you seen in this field? What do you predict over the next ten years?

- What does your average day/week/month/quarter look like?

- Describe the best part of your job and the most challenging.

- Would you choose this career again? Why or why not?

- Do you know anyone who entered this field as a next career? What is your perception of the individual's challenges, strengths, weaknesses, and acceptance among colleagues?

Can you introduce me? Alternatively: What challenges and opportunities do you see for someone in my shoes? What skills or knowledge might help me get up to speed most quickly; to succeed, or to fail?

*Step Three.* Ask yourself, "What do I want school to do for me?" When asked why you are returning to school, this is the answer that matters the most. Those seriously considering a return to school hold at least one explicit or implicit belief about what school will do for them. Many believe it will fulfill a lifelong dream to contribute to the world in a certain way. Some hope to bring life to long-held academic or professional goals. Others anticipate additional education will increase job stability, provide greater flexibility and work/family balance, or increase personal satisfaction. A wise academic and next-career choice is one that honors your answer.

And speaking of your answer…this is the time to identify what you want out of this. As active adults it is easy to lose track of one's own interests and instead parrot what someone else (or the world) believes should be the result of your schooling and next career. If we inadvertently pursue someone else's vision, the post-graduation result can be a worn-out, confused individual who wonders, "Is this all there is?" Take care to make sure you aren't actually chasing someone else's potential, someone else's dream, someone else's desired outcome (e.g., an executive paycheck). Although a sensible academic and next-career choice considers the affect on others, it starts with a foundation that honors your goals, your dreams, and your desired outcome for this educational pursuit (which may or may not include big bucks in the top five most important outcomes list).

What are reasonable expectations? Identify tangible outcomes specific to the educational experience you decide to pursue. These may include the opportunity to learn something new or add a credential to your resume. Look out for vague expectations. A degree or certificate may open doors to a new career but qualities such as happiness and financial stability are as much a result of your own attitude and hard work as is the diploma.

Whatever it is you want school to do for you, name it and frame it. Literally. Hang it on your wall. Carry it on a slip of paper in your wallet. Tape it to your bathroom mirror. Make it the wallpaper for your cell phone or laptop. Make sure you see it several times a day. Update these reminders as your goals change along the way. Always know your own expectations for the other side of this degree. As the old saying goes, "If you don't know where you're going, any road will get you there" (Lewis Carroll).

## RESPONSIBLE FUNDING

Retraining costs time and money (and if time is money, then retraining actually costs money plus more money…but enough math for the moment). Money has two primary components 1) the actual funds (getting them and spending them), and 2) money-related emotions (that cling to money decisions like bits of plastic wrap). The first is fact-based. Either the funds exist or they don't. The second is wherein the power lies. The power to decide if, when, where, and on what to spend (or save) the actual funds; and, the power to label the decision as wise or foolish long after the money is gone.

### Emotions and Buying

The emotional aspect of financing school rarely receives the consideration it deserves in the back-to-school equation. No matter what type of program you are considering, education costs money that could be used on something else; or for someone else. Even with cash in the bank for tuition and living expenses, it is rational to ask yourself if, in the long run, the funds might be better spent on, oh I don't know, a trip to Hawaii, or (seriously speaking), saved for a house or retirement.

School isn't the answer to all life's challenges. Go back to the previous section of this chapter and review what you want the educational experience and new career to do for you. How does the potential cost of school compare with the personal value of reaching your current goal? The value here is the long term psychological value to you rather than a predicted marketplace value of a specific degree. And yes, this is impossible to answer for sure, but, it is good to consider the question.

The metaphor I use to answer this question is that of buying a new car. I've had a lot of old clunkers in my day so when I buy a new car I expect it to work, drive me where I want to go, behave in accordance with the manufacturer's claims, and last five to ten years. If the car meets my criteria, I compare the cost of the car with the value I place on my four criteria. A thumbs up results in a purchase. A thumbs down leads to more shopping.

This is the same process that occurs when you label an item as either too expensive or a real deal. The trick with education is that the value is hard to define. The best you can do is know what you want and then talk to those who have done it. The informational interview questions in the prior section are a good place to start.

If predictions for multiple careers in one's lifetime are true, ten years is about what you can expect of a next career—fifteen if you're lucky. When I compare educational costs with my expectations for what it will bring, I use a modified car-purchase analysis. I ask myself if, for this price, the educational credential will 1) be recognized and valuable to employers, 2) help me meet a personal and/or career goal, 3) teach me to perform the skills claimed by the marketing materials, and 4) last five to ten years. It is a bonus if the credential plus experience may help build my next career.

## Emotions and Borrowing

Next, if you plan to borrow money for tuition or expenses, take time to think about the emotional elements of acquiring and spending these funds. Student loans can be a fine idea but should be evaluated in light of your long-range financial goals. Otherwise, there can be a big surprise down the road—and not one of those happy, fun surprises!

Do not automatically rely on student loans without reviewing options or the burden of long term payments. This is money that must be paid back. As of this writing, student loan debt does not go away in bankruptcy. Even if you go belly-up and are living in a van down by the river, the student loan collectors will find you.

College financial aid officers can point you in the direction of many options, but keep in mind two important points: the financial aid officers' job is to help you find all the money you need to come to their institution, and they don't have to pay back your loans. Student loan funds quickly begin to feel like play money to students rather than actual dollars you owe, making it easy to lose sight of the total debt load being incurred. The best financial aid officers can help you choose loans in line with your likely income after graduation. Here are a few simple steps to help your post-graduation financial surprises be happy ones.

Before accepting a loan know:

- Minimum monthly payment

- Interest rate (fixed only, please)

- When the first payment is due (e.g., immediately upon taking out the loan, sometime after graduation, when your course load is reduced to part-time).

Each time a family member went to school. I created a student loan tracking chart. An example using fictitious data is on the next page. The body of the chart tracks the details. The bottom line, literally, provides the bottom line—total debt and estimated minimum monthly payment to date. The impact of seeing one's current debt load can provide perspective and encourage emotionally and financially healthy decisions regarding additional debt.

Before each semester, look at the bottom line of your chart and ask yourself these questions using your own numbers. Your answers will depend on your unique combination of facts and feelings.

- How do I feel about carrying more than $13,500 in debt in order to achieve my educational goals? ($13,500 has already been incurred; the decision at this point is whether or not to incur additional debt.)

- If a new job doesn't come along immediately after graduation, how will loan payments of more than $177.21 per month impact my current budget and lifestyle? (Same caveat as above)

# Student Loan Tracking Chart

NOTE: The figures are not based on actual loan details. Lender websites offer calculators to determine accurate payment amounts based on specific loan details.

| Loan Amount | Date Taken | Minimum Payment (monthly) | Interest Rate | Term (yrs.) | Due |
|---|---|---|---|---|---|
| $5,000 | Fall 2009 | $57.54 | 6.8% | 10 | 6 mos after graduate |
| $2,500 | Winter 2010 | $50 | 7.25% | 5 | If not FT student |
| $6,000 | Spring 2010 | $69.67 | 7% | 10 | Interest |
| Total = $13,500 | | Total = $177.21 | | | |

*Facts* may include current income, predicted post-graduate income, family responsibilities and near-term purchase plans that include debt (e.g., car, home, medical expenses, office set-up, and children's education). Use caution when estimating post-graduate income, especially in the early years.

*Emotions* may include a mix of pride ("I'm worth it!"), vision ("This goal is worth it!"), fear ("I'm spending how much?!"), personal risk tolerance ("I'm OK risking $X to get this degree.") and hope ("The long term payback will be well worth it."). Most importantly, try to avoid the blind-eye approach to debt incursion.

It is a healthy sign if you feel uneasy about taking on more debt. Step back, take a deep breath, and review your financial options. Take stock of your goals in light of current market conditions and other facts. Then make a decision and go forward with confidence. Taking a little time each semester to check-in with the factual and emotional components of your financial choices will help you make wise decisions along the way.

The next page lays out a chart with ten funding questions to consider. This chart is followed by another containing sample answers. Both charts are available for download at the Back to School for Grownups website (http://backtoschoolforgrownups.com).

To be clear, student loans are an amazing benefit. Reflecting on federally subsidized loans a favorite student of mine from Liberia said, "What a wonderful government that says, 'Here. Take this money that I will lend you to become educated and better yourself and society!'" For many, educational loans provide a bridge to opportunities that can change the lives of the student, their family and those they serve. Imagine how few doctors or teachers or social workers there would be if higher education was available on a cash-only basis! Don't let the financial piece indefinitely stall your decision. But move forward with your eyes open.

## Ten Funding Questions to Consider

| | | |
|---|---|---|
| 1. | How much are you willing to invest by committing to loans? | |
| 2. | How much savings can you comfortably spend? | |
| 3. | How much tuition funding is available from your employer per year? Check with your employee handbook or human resource department for details. | |
| 4. | How long, if at all, do you expect to be under-employed (i.e. internships, part-time work during school) or unemployed? Allow for full-time attendance and time between graduation and finding a new job. | |
| 5. | How do you plan to fund your living expenses during this time? (If you don't know your average monthly expenses estimate them, then confirm.) | |
| 6. | What is your gut feel for the total monetary cost you are willing to invest for this educational program? (cash and loans) | |
| 7. | What is your gut feel for the time you can invest being in transition? Consider two types of time 1) personal time away from friends, family, and your regular activities, and 2) time spent rebuilding the new career. | |
| 8. | What salary level do you need in your second career? For how long (years)? | |
| 9. | What trade-offs can allow you to take a lower salary for a period of time (e.g., less travel, fewer hours, more flexibility, growth opportunities, or improved benefits)? | |
| 10. | Assume you will start at the bottom of the pay scale. What is the range? Estimate low. If you get a plum job with big bucks I am certain you will find a use for the "extra" money. If not, send it to the charity of your choice. Either way, everybody wins. | |

# Sample Answers to Ten Funding Questions

| Question | Commentary | Sample answer |
|---|---|---|
| 1. How much to commit to in loans? | A rule of thumb is *one year's salary* using the starting salary range for new graduates. | $$$ |
| 2. Savings you can comfortably contribute to reduce loan debt. | Savings? Many adults take a "real time" approach by *not spending*. It is amazing how little one can live on for a short time and still be sane. Adopting a student lifestyle at age forty-plus can also be fun (student discounts, youth hostels). The looks alone are worth it. | Daily decisions. Look for ways to cut corners (used books) or not spend at all; maximize credits taken per semester to graduate early. |
| 3. Tuition funds available from employer per year. | If these funds are available to you, USE THEM! This may be FREE MONEY, but read the policy for details such as grade minimums. | $ |
| 4. How long, if at all, do you expect to be under-employed or unemployed? | This is a wildcard. Even if you are working full-time while attending school you may consider taking time off for an internship or to take an entry-level position as you transition to the new career. Keep this in the back of your mind as a consideration. | X months |
| 5. What options do you have to fund your living expenses if you reduce or leave your current employment? | Be creative. Ask about unusual scholarships or grants. Talk to friends who went back to school, professors, librarians, industry organizations, church or social groups; check websites but don't pay for lists. Avoid spam emails and fraudulent scholarship schemes. Balance the application's complexity & time to complete with the chance to receive the award. | |

*continued on next page*

55

| | | |
|---|---|---|
| 6. What is your gut feel for the total monetary cost you are willing to invest for the perceived benefit of this educational program? | Rather than nailing down a precise number, approach this like any major purchase—say, a vehicle. Identify your needs and wants (e.g., is the heater-and-keys version sufficient or are you looking to impress your neighbors?). Shop around. Compare prices, reputation and track record for placing graduates. Talk to working graduates. | Does the cost to attend this school feel worth the time, money, and possible benefit *to you* in the end? |
| 7. What is your gut feel for the time you can invest being in transition? | Many adults hope to be back on track as soon as possible with the new career (not necessarily at the same salary but back on track to get there). | Look for work in the new field during school, even as an intern or clerk. |
| 8. What salary level do you need? For how long (years)? | Distinguish between "need" and "would really like to make." Your answers may help clarify a specialty area or major. | To start, use an average industry salary for ten years full-time and more time for part-time. |
| 9. Are there trade-offs you can make to take a lower salary for a period of time? | Think creatively. Tangible, intangible, or personal. For example, switching to a company with tuition benefits may be worth a reduced starting salary. Others are willing to take a pay cut to trade a high stress career for one with fewer demands. | Maybe there are, but maybe you just need a change. |
| 10. Will you likely start at the bottom of the pay scale for the new position (assume yes!)? What is the range? Estimate low. | ERR ON THE LOW SIDE! Too many adults assume prior experience equals high salary. Don't be fooled. Without an established pathway to the new career or great fortune, you will start at the bottom with the rest of us. You may rise more quickly – or not. A meteoric rise in any career is about as common as, well, meteors. | Mitigate the risk of low-ball offers by gaining experience with internships while you are still a student. After graduation look for opportunities with acceptable compensation and great mentoring. |

# WHAT DO THE HIGHER EDUCATION PROFESSIONALS SAY?

Chapter Three began with six self-described characteristics from successful adult students. The final section of this chapter presents opinions from the other side of the table. In the fall of 2009 a survey was sent to approximately 300 professionals at community colleges, career colleges, public and private universities, technical schools and certificate programs. Forty-four responses were received. Each respondent or department was selected based on their involvement with adult learners. The intent of the survey was to gain insight from professors, deans, and administrators on the most important predictors of success (and faltering) they have witnessed in returning adult students. The data collected through this nonscientific survey provides a snapshot from forty-four professionals from across the country. A full report follows Chapter Seven in the Appendix.

Participants were asked the following questions:

1.  Have you seen a growth in the number of adult students returning to school? If yes, do you think this trend will continue? Why?

2.  In your experience, what are the three most common characteristics of successful returning adult students? (Participants ranked three from a group of characteristics and had the option to write in a response not found on the list.)

3.  Based on your experience, what do you believe to be the three most common derailers for returning adult students? (Participants ranked three from a group of characteristics and had the option to write in a response not found on the list.)

4.  What one thing should adult students returning to school know?

Keeping in mind the nonscientific nature of the study and the relatively small numbers, here is what the higher education respondents said:

Ninety-one percent of respondents have seen a growth in the number of adults returning to school. Thirty-five respondents provided their thoughts on whether they think this trend will continue and why (full responses are in the Appendix). Several themes emerged:

- Challenging economic conditions marked by layoffs and high unemployment.

- Increases in life expectancy support lifelong learning and multiple occupational interests.

- Current jobs require new skills and knowledge.

- Personal interest and readiness.

Respondents were asked to select three characteristics common among successful students and then rank the three characteristics as most common, second most common, and third most common. Commitment was identified most often as the number one characteristic of successful students. Time-Management Skills received the most total votes across all three rankings, followed closely by Perseverance and Commitment. Given the small numbers and razor-thin differences, it is fair to say that successful students are like to demonstrate all three. The more interesting data followed.

Two factors tied for the next total-votes position: Willingness to Ask for Help and Family Support. Although it received a single vote as the number one most common characteristic of successful students, Family Support received the highest score for the number two ranking. In other words, it is unlikely that family support is enough to drive success if the student lacks personal commitment, perseverance and time-management skills. However, if the student has the personal characteristics indicative of success, it is likely there is some form of family cheering them on in the background.

Are you concerned about your ability to be an "A" student? Rest easy. NO ONE, not one respondent ranked being an "A" student among the top three characteristics common among successful adult students.

Next, respondents were asked to rank the top three characteristics most common among students who were derailed from their studies. The term "derailed" was used intentionally rather than something such as "failure." Adult students who do the work needed to return to school are less likely than young students to drop out because the dog ate their homework or they partied too hard to study (Poor Grades only received one vote in this section.) Working adults have too much invested and too much at stake to mess around.

Financial Issues and Unexpected Events received the most votes across all three rankings as well as the numbers one, two, and three most common derailer positions. Family Complications was close behind. These respondents would likely suggest students take time to think through the financial aspect of school before jumping in—and have a plan for working through unexpected events. One classmate was called to active duty several weeks before graduation. While he couldn't ignore the call, he knew this might happen and was ready to work closely with the school to ensure a quick re-entry to complete his education upon his return. Other events are less predictable. Either way, our experts see this as a top reason for student derailment. See Chapter Four for further discussion on this topic.

Are you concerned about getting along with classmates half your age? Generational Divide with Other Students scores a big zero in this survey. Not one respondent ranked it among the top three reasons for student derailment. So dust off your old backpack, get out your albums and rock on. Peace.

Finally, respondents were given the opportunity to add anything else they wished. This was their chance to tell you, the potential next student in their classroom, what you should know when you return to school. Their statements are priceless. I encourage you to read each of their remarks in the Appendix for insight or a shot of inspiration. I've selected a few to highlight:

- "This is the time to prepare for that career you always wanted. Make the most of your time on campus. Use the resources; make connections; claim your education."

- "That "smart" is what you become when you are determined to learn and willing to ask for help."

- "They are capable of much more than they can imagine."

- "There is no perfect time to start back in school. Life will always be busy. The longer you wait to jump in, the longer it will be before you graduate!"

## Summary

By now you are well down the path to returning to school. In Chapter Three you took a good look at yourself and your pocketbook. You looked closely at the occupational field of interest to you. You learned what returning students say it takes to succeed and you read the perspective of higher educational professionals. You are confident in your abilities and your study area choice. Going back to school is what you want to do. All that stands between you and the classroom is finding the school and program you want, making it happen (admission and money), and mentally preparing for that first day. Welcome to Chapter Four.

# Chapter Four

# Going Back To School

*"Smart is what you become when you are determined to learn and willing to ask for help."*

Chapter Four describes the three remaining steps in your back-to-school journey. The first is to identify the academic model that best meets your needs. This chapter begins with brief definitions of choices for today's student. Does a certificate program meet your needs or do you want a full-fledged degree? Do you prefer online or face-to-face classes? Is a traditional environment best for your learning style or would nontraditional be preferable? Once you know the model you want it will be easier to identify a specific school and program to target. By the end of the first section you will have information to make those decisions.

Now that you've identified the program you want, the next step is to gain acceptance. The middle section of Chapter Four offers insight on prerequisites, effective applications and getting your name on the "accepted" list. This chapter ends with a few words of advice about final preparations for that long-awaited first day of class.

# Finding the Right Program

Today's academic environment is full of choices. Many excellent programs are available that didn't exist when a lot of us graduated from high school. Certificate and short-term training programs provide targeted learning. Weekend and evening programs offer degree and nondegree options for working adults. Technology makes it possible to earn a number of bachelor's, master's or even doctorate degrees without leaving your home—and still interact with classmates from around the world. This section provides an overview of basic options available in today's learning environment.

## Degree or Certificate Programs

In general, formal educational programs fall into two broad categories: degree programs and certificate programs. Many jobs require a college degree. Some require only a specialized certificate. Others require both (i.e., higher level positions in accounting may require a bachelor's degree and Certified Public Accountant (CPA) certification). Talk to hiring professionals in your field of interest. What educational credentials are required? What credentials set a candidate apart from the crowd?

So what is a degree? Webster's Dictionary defines the word degree as "a title conferred on students by a college, university, or professional school (e.g., law school, medical school, school of psychiatry) on completion of a program of study." A degree is a recognized measurement of educational quantity (number of credits earned). Students earn a title that starts with a general label (associate's, bachelor's, master's, doctorate, and so forth) and ends with a topic of study (nursing, archeology, English, math). Fancy schools may add specifics (associate's degree in fourteenth-century English literature). Degree programs come in various lengths (two-year, three-year, six-year, and then all bets are off). Many fast-track programs reduce those time frames for adults with prior college credit or who are just in a hurry.

Certificate programs are typically short term educational options. Most certificate training programs take between a month and two years to complete. Some certificates can only be acquired after degree completion. Others require no formal training beyond high school. Many certificates are earned by passing a national exam recognized by the relevant professional organization. Certificates serve as evidence that the recipient has specialized skill gained through training and/or experience in a specific type of work (e.g., welding, Pilates instructor, personal coaching).

Certificates can kick-off a new profession or enhance an established specialty area (e.g., senior professional in human resources (HR), C++ certification, mini-masters of business administration (MBA) in nonprofit management). Certificate holders often have letters behind their names that professionals in their field recognize such as CMT (certified massage therapist) and CISSP (certified information systems security professional).

Certificate programs are specific and narrowly focused. Degree programs are general and broadly focused. Whereas a certificate may provide an entry to a certain type of position, a college degree may provide the breadth of knowledge needed to allow for career opportunities in an entire field and beyond.

An undergraduate degree from an accredited school is a prerequisite for graduate work. For many graduate programs, the specific degree is not as important as the fact that the applicant has a degree. To be on the safe side, if you are returning to complete an undergraduate degree and think you may continue on to earn an advanced degree, check the application requirements in two or three graduate programs to make sure you keep your options open. The fourteenth-century English literature degree may be a perfect foundation for a master's in secondary education but might be a stretch if your sights are set on a graduate program in nuclear physics.

Another benefit of a college degree is that once you have earned it, it is yours. No one can take it away—ever. Many certificate programs require recipients to take continuing education courses, retest at certain intervals, and pay annual membership fees in approved professional organizations. Failure to meet these post-certification requirements may result in loss of one's certification.

In terms of payback, the monetary value of a degree over a lifetime is well established, whereas little has been documented about certificate-only programs. However, if you already have a degree and wish to target a career for which there is a valued certification program, the latter may be a more efficient route.

The best choice for you is the one that helps you get where you want to go at this point in your life. Each type of program is valid and useful. The best choice depends on your goals. The chart below briefly describes typical characteristic and points to consider for each type of program.

Karin is a good example. She is deciding between a degree and a certificate programs. Karin has a bachelor's degree in art. She worked as a human resource assistant at a museum for the past ten years to supplement sales of her artwork. As an HR assistant, Karin discovered her gift for working with numbers and explaining complex benefit programs to people. Plus, the starving artist life is less attractive with each passing day.

## DEGREE AND CERTIFICATE PROGRAM COMPARISON CHART

| | Degree Programs | Certificate Programs |
|---|---|---|
| **Characteristics** | • Conferred by colleges and universities.<br>• Offered through a college or university, typically accredited.<br>• Core set of required courses plus set number of electives.<br>• Intent is to educate the whole person. | • Conferred by professional trade organizations.<br>• Can be offered on-site at a workplace, in a college setting, online, or at industry training centers.<br>• Curriculum targeted to a skill or knowledge set.<br>• Intent is to train the individual to perform a specific task or job. This can be as specific as pipe-fitter or as broad as senior professional in HR. |
| **Points to Consider** | • Generally understood and recognized by employers.<br>• Provides broad perspective.<br>• Typically one to six years. An associate's degree is two years, undergraduate is four, graduate school is two to three, law school is three. Medical school and doctorate degrees are more. Fast track programs are less.<br>• Required for many jobs. Required for many advanced educational programs including many certificate programs. | • Recognition varies.<br>• Targeted to a specific skill or knowledge base.<br>• Short term.<br>• May be required in addition to a degree, may be combined with experience in place of a degree or stand alone as evidence of training to perform a specific task. |

Karin wants to become a benefits specialist for small- to mid-sized nonprofit organizations. She has no aspirations to oversee an entire HR department or move to the for-profit sector. Karin's goal may be best met through a nationally recognized certificate program in employee benefits administration. However, if she wants to keep her options open for the long term, she would be wise to consider graduate degree programs in human resources. In two years or fewer she could gain the skills to be employable as a benefits specialist while attaining the credentials for upward movement at a later time. The choice is hers.

## Online or Face-to-Face

A decision few returning students faced the first time around was whether to attend classes in person or electronically (a.k.a., virtually). The image of going to school is typically one of students in desks with a teacher up front. One literally *goes to* the school. Technological advances have expanded the classroom walls to the ends of the earth, or at least to wherever there is an internet connection.

Having the option to take coursework online doesn't mean it is the best alternative for each individual. In fact, my position as the face-to-face professor in an MBA program exists because the original all-online program did not meet the academic needs of some students. Today, the school offers a blended model combining online and face-to-face courses.

The chart on the next page lists a few advantages and challenges for online and face-to-face formats. What comes to mind as you read through this chart? Add your own concerns or ideas in the margin.

If you aren't sure if online courses are for you, try taking a community education course online and see how it goes. These are inexpensive, interesting, and short. If you found it difficult to complete the work, think twice before signing up for an all-online program. If your only option is an all-online program, use your experience with the community education course to identify areas where you need to develop strategies in order to succeed. An example might be creating a schedule for completion of assignments in order to stay on task.

## ADVANTAGES AND CHALLENGES
## FOR ONLINE AND FACE-TO-FACE FORMATS

| | Online Courses | Face-to-Face Courses |
|---|---|---|
| **Advantages** | • Available anywhere there is an internet connection.<br>• Online student/student and student/faculty exchanges may be more candid and in-depth, allowing for increased group sharing. | • Camaraderie among classmates facilitates networking, personal support, and group expectation for performance.<br>• Group dynamics include verbal and nonverbal responses. |
| **Challenges** | • Requires significant self-discipline to complete assignments and be mentally present during "live" online sessions.<br>• Lack of face-to-face connection with peers may lead to feelings of isolation and reduced motivation for course or program. | • Must be physically present.<br>• Course is offered at a specified day and time. |

## Traditional or Nontraditional

Degree programs may be further characterized as traditional or nontraditional. Traditional programs are what typically come to mind when one imagines going to college. Classes occur in classrooms on a campus with a library, student center, and trees. Most classes are scheduled during the day. Required courses are scheduled with the assumption that students are in full-time attendance. Course content and assignments are based on scholarly research and theory, with consistency semester to semester. Students attend lectures, turn in assignments, take exams, and receive grades. The typical student is between eighteen to twenty-five years old with no professional work experience. Student organizations and services are geared toward individuals in this age range.

Nontraditional programs encompass everything else. Coursework may be completed in the classroom, online, or in a combination of online and face-to-face courses. Many classes are scheduled in the evening or on weekends. A growing number of accredited traditional schools are offering weekend-only degree programs in

66

many fields including law, business, and health care. Courses may be held on a traditional campus, at a work site, in an office building or conference center, or in the field—literally. For example, classes for a specialized MBA in winery management are held online and on-site around the world at renowned wineries.

Course content in nontraditional programs may emphasize practical, hands-on application of the topic. Internships may be part of the curriculum or strongly encouraged. Nontraditional programs schedule the required courses with part-time students in mind. College administrative functions such as admissions, libraries, career services, and counseling may include programs designed for the returning adult student. Student ages range from the fourteen-year-old genius to the ninety-five-year-old grandma, although most fall in the twenty-five to sixty-five age range. Many have professional work experience. Most bring a wealth of life experience to the classroom.

Traditional programs are the mainstay of higher education. However, many adults can't commit the daytime hours necessary to attend a full-time traditional program, particularly when completion requires multiple years of coursework. Nontraditional programs open academic possibilities to these students. Today, many colleges and universities offer elements of traditional and nontraditional programs to meet the needs of a growing student population. From a personal perspective, the option to attend a nontraditional college made it possible for me to complete an undergraduate degree while working and parenting small children.

## Putting It All Together

As you look at certificate and degree programs, online or face-to-face, traditional and nontraditional programs, think about what approach best matches your educational goals, learning style, personality, and personal situation. Looking for a simple four-step plan to help you choose a program? Keep reading.

### FOUR-STEP PROGRAM COMPARISON CHART

1. Identify two to five specific programs that offer the education you want.
2. Fill in the details for each program in the top half of the following chart.
3. Use the bottom half to list qualities that are important to

you. For example, how does the school support returning adult students? (Samples provided below).

4. Apply to the program(s) that best fits your needs.

## Four-Step Program Comparison Chart

Note: These are common items students use to compare programs. Replace with items important to you.

| Basic Information | | | | | |
|---|---|---|---|---|---|
| School name | Tuition & books cost per year | Time to finish all courses | Entrance exams and other reqmts | Degree or certificate to be earned | Student/ teacher ratio (or something of show-stopper importance to you) |
| First School | | | | | |
| Second School | | | | | |
| Third School | | | | | |
| Fourth School | | | | | |

| More Stuff That is Important to You | | | | | |
|---|---|---|---|---|---|
| (this example chose indicators of being adult student friendly) | | | | | |
| School name | Average age of student body | Library hours and off-site access | Scheduling options and flexibility | Student activities and administrative support geared toward next-career seekers | Other issues important to you (parking, daycare, career transition support) |
| First School | | | | | |
| Second School | | | | | |
| Third School | | | | | |
| Fourth School | | | | | |

## FOUR-STEP PROGRAM COMPARISON CHART
### Example

| Basic Information | | | | |
|---|---|---|---|---|
| **Program** | **Tuition & books cost/yr** | **Length of program** | **Entrance rqmts** | **Degree or certificate** |
| Big State College | $$$$ per year | Four years, full-time | Transcript from HS, SAT scores, essay, recommendations | BA |
| Cool Private College | $$$$$$ per year | Four years, full-time | Competitive | BA |
| Nearby Community College | $$$ per year | Two years | | Associate's degree |
| REC Institute | $$$$ paid at once | One year | None | Certificate only |

| More Stuff That is Important to You | | | | |
|---|---|---|---|---|
| **Program** | **Student body avg age** | **Library access** | **Scheduling options and flexibility** | **Support for next-career seekers** |
| Big State College | Twenty-five | Building open 8 a.m. to midnight | Mostly daytime courses. | One part-time career counselor for entire school. |
| Cool Private College | Thirty-eight | Online only | Day and evening options. | School geared toward returning adult students. |
| Nearby Community College | Thirty-four | 8 a.m. to 10 p.m. | Many class schedule options. | Limited |
| AAKT Institute | Forty-five | No library | Offered three times a year. | Through professional organization |

## Making it Happen

You've chosen to pursue a certificate or a degree program, made the decision to go full-time or part-time, identified whether to look for traditional or nontraditional programs, and determined if online or face-to-face courses fit your needs. Armed with this information, you've identified three to five specific programs that meet your goals. The next step is gaining admission. This section looks at three aspects of the admissions process: prerequisites, the application process itself and increasing your chance to get in.

### Prerequisites

A prerequisite is something that is required in advance or before something else can occur. Prerequisites for certificate and degree programs may include experience in the field of study, attainment of junior-level certificates or degrees, or successful completion of specific coursework. With rare exception, applicants must complete program prerequisites before beginning a course of study. Individuals who seek certification by examination must present evidence of prerequisite completion before they are allowed to sit for the exam. If you are making a significant shift from your first career, prerequisites can also prepare you for successful study in the new field.

For example, Brian, an aspiring musician with a degree in international relations, sustained a career-changing injury. After exploring new career options he chose to pursue a master's degree in physical therapy. However, his undergraduate studies did not include coursework in health-related areas. Consequently, before the physical therapy program would consider his application, Brian was required to complete three prerequisite courses with a grade of B or higher in biology, anatomy, and statistics. Brian worked with the school to identify academic options to meet these requirements in an efficient, cost-effective manner. In the end, Brian was able to take one class online, another through a community college, and the third at the college where he hoped to study physical therapy.

The story of Brian brings up an important point about graduate school. Many graduate programs accept candidates with undergraduate degrees from other disciplines as long as specific prerequisites are met. For example, medical schools no longer limit acceptance to math and science undergraduates. However, medical schools do have a long list of math and science prerequisites. Likewise, MBA programs typically require undergraduate statistics and economics courses. Thus, if you have a bachelor's degree in art and want to pursue an MBA, you won't need to earn a second undergraduate degree first. But you will need to identify and complete any prerequisite courses.

But why not take the time to get another undergraduate degree? Answer: economics. Why spend several more years and tons more money if prerequisites are sufficient and you can probably get a master's degree in less time? Prerequisites are your friends.

Identify the prerequisites for your program of interest by checking the school's website or application materials. If that fails, call the admissions department and ask. Proof that you have met the prerequisites will be required as part of your application. Often this is in the form of an official transcript or notarized form. Ask the school what they require as proof. Make sure you allow ample time for the paperwork to be processed by the institution holding the document, and for the document to be received by you and submitted before the application deadline.

## Application Process

Each school (and sometimes each program within a school) has its own application process. The process can be complex, time-consuming, and confusing. In addition to the standard application form, many schools require an essay, reference letters, transcripts of prior academic work, or other evidence you have met all requirements and prerequisites. Only then can you be considered for admission to the program. Entrance tests, if required, can range from basic competency tests designed by the school to standardized tests such as the Scholastic Aptitude Test (SAT), Graduate Record Examination (GRE), Graduate Management Admission Test (GMAT), Law School Admission Test (LSAT), or Medical College Admission Test (MCAT). Artistic, craftsman, or other hands-on, creative programs may also require an audition or portfolio of your work. Further, there are two distinct but interconnected application processes: application for admission and application for financial aid.

### Application for admission

In recent years a number of colleges agreed to accept a single online form that allows prospective students to apply to more than one school at roughly the same time. However, don't assume this is considered what schools call a "completed application," or puts you in a competitive position with others who personalized their applications for each school. If this is your dream school, go the extra mile to make sure your application is competitive.

Further, applications that are sloppy, incomplete, or fail to comply with directions go to the bottom of the pile. In this sense, school applications are similar to job applications. Putting your best foot forward increases the chance your application will make it to the next stage of the process.

Allow plenty of time to complete each application. Start well in advance of deadlines. Give yourself time to write and edit entrance essays. Also, remember you may be requesting transcripts, letters of recommendations, and copies of test scores or government documentation (for foreign study). Each involves people—who get sick, go on vacation, and get behind. Each step takes time. ALL of these items or whatever is relevant to your specific program are part of a "completed application." Given the high volume of applicants to many programs, only fully completed applications are considered for admission to most programs.

*Application for financial aid*

Once your application for admission is complete, financial aid applications are the next documents to prepare. Some schools require students to submit financial aid forms with a completed application for admission. Others have specific deadlines for various school-sponsored or government-sponsored financial aid. In addition to the standard federal forms such as the Free Application for Federal Student Aid (FAFSA) many schools have their own application for financial aid. Identify the application forms your school requires and all relevant deadlines.

Financial aid comes in two broad forms that typically require separate applications: money that must be paid back (e.g., student loans), and everything else. Scholarships and grants typically fall into the latter category, although not always. Some programs match applicants with funding as their applications are reviewed for admission. This is especially true for nonloan or scholarship and grant funds. Funding options vary by school, are typically competitive, and may include tuition discounts in the form of merit scholarships, academic department awards, or alumni or friend-of-the-school scholarships. However, once the money is gone it is indeed gone. Ask your school how early you can submit an application for financial aid. It is good to be in the front of this line if possible.

Additional funding may be available through outside organizations such as the National Garden Club; a professional organization related to your field of study such as the International Association of Privacy Professionals; or competitions funded by corporate sponsors such as Coca-Cola or Best Buy. Each has its own application process, forms, and deadlines.

Corporate tuition reimbursement funds may be available as another source of educational money. The application process to receive these funds may be as simple as making a request to your manager. It is more likely to require multiple approvals and possibly an executive sign-off. Check program details. Standard practice is to release the funds after satisfactory course completion (hence the term "reimbursement"), which means you'll need to locate money up front for the class. In addition, some organizations require payback of the funds if you leave the company within a specific timeframe (voluntarily or not).

Financial aid applications must be timely, neat, and painstakingly accurate. All financial aid forms require details about your personal financial life such as taxes, savings, retirement, income, and so forth. The application may also require an essay, or, in the case of competitions, some creative pursuit such as a video of why you deserve the scholarship. As with your admissions application, keep track of each financial aid application to ensure you have done everything possible to allow the other side to say, "Hey, let's give this person some money!"

*Keeping on track*

Some people find it helpful to create a chart that identifies specific application requirements to ensure every detail is addressed on time, and in the manner requested. This chart can double as a model for tracking complex homework assignments later on. Each step of the process is tracked with specifics such as date completed and highlights of relevant conversations (e.g., ordered transcript from U on June 30; spoke with Seth who said it would be mailed first class in three business days).

The next three pages include three admissions application examples, two for certificate programs and one for a degree program. The same model can be used to track requirements for specific financial aid application requirements. These charts neither reflect the general requirements for similar applications nor all the requirements for any one specific process. In reality, there are more steps and substeps to each application process. If the model is helpful, adjust the details according to the requirements of your program.

## ADMISSIONS APPLICATION REQUIREMENT TRACKING
### THREE MODELS USING FICTITIOUS DATA

### Certificate Program Example
Certificate in Welding at CircleSaw Institute
Eighteen-month program

| Admissions Task | Status | Notes |
|---|---|---|
| Application deadline November 15 for admission in January. | Decide if I'm going to shoot for January admission or wait until spring. | Talk to boss and check home schedule. |
| Talk to admissions rep. | Met with Max Wilson on 7/15. | Submit soon! Max suggested getting my boss and a former instructor to send recommendation letters for my admissions file. |
| Order high school transcript. | Contacted Central HS; Betty is sending transcript this week. | First I need to send them a check for $5 with a note signed by me. (Done) |
| Order transcript from prior college. | Contacted Blue Heron Community College, talked to Hank. | Online order form, use credit card for $3 fee. (Done) |
| Complete and submit online application. | Need to do! | Need Blue Heron address; need to decide if using VA benefits. |
| Confirm application is complete and was received. | Call Max one week after submitting online application. | Email thanks to Max for all his help. |

74

# Degree Program Example
MBA at Sparkle University

| Admissions Task | Status | Notes |
|---|---|---|
| Application deadline is March 1 for fall admission. | In process. | Personal goal: submit completed application by November 1. |
| Register and take GMAT. | Registered June 12 for August 3 exam. | NEED TO STUDY. |
| Ask two professors or managers to recommend me. | Ray hasn't responded. Salina said yes. Sent her the form on July 2. | If can't find Ray by August 1, contact Sam. |
| Complete online application. | Still to do. | Paper application must include $60, online is free. |
| Request transcripts from schools attended. Schools must use Sparkle's form from the application. | Sent to Sunflower U, Eastwest Community College and Heffer Grad School on July 10. | Submit in sealed envelopes signed by a university official. Send directly to Sparkle. |
| Include current resume in application. | Polish by September 15. | Add recent promotion and relevant volunteer work. |
| Essay questions. | Draft by September 1. Have Sarah review and comment. | Complete essay questions by October 15. |

# Certification by Exam Only Example
## Professional in Human Resources

| Admissions Task | Status | Notes |
|---|---|---|
| Registration deadline is October 9 to sit for December or January exam. | Need to register. | Work on registration this month. |
| Locate requirements. | Need to register on website to see requirements and complete application to sit for exam. | Do right away so I know if I am OK or short of requirements. |
| Locate study materials and prep course, purchase or register. | Mary and Teresa took this last year. Ask to borrow their materials and if they took the course. | Decide if taking prep course. |
| Locate test site. | Society for HR Management (SHRM) website link. | Test is available during an 8-week block of time. |
| Register for exam. | SHRM website link. | |
| Schedule study time. | For six weeks, an hour a day plus class if I take it. | Find someone to take notes for travel week. |
| Take exam. | Plan to take the first week in December. | Cross fingers. |

Aspiring students joke that the college application process is actually a test given by the admissions staff to determine an applicant's ability to complete homework that is required in the program. Although not completely accurate, consider these similarities:

- Neither homework nor the application process are inherently fun but must be done on time and comply with precise directions that aren't always logical.

- Stuff we learned in grade school including neatness, accuracy, and attention to detail can affect the desired outcome.

- Effective completion stands between you and your goal.

Practically speaking, from a decision-maker's perspective, a sloppy or incomplete application takes more time to process. Plus, it implies the applicant will be sloppy and incomplete with studies and careless with funding. Depending on how many applications the reviewer has read that day, and how many more are still in the pile, the application may not be given a second thought. Take the time to make sure your application doesn't get rejected for these correctable reasons.

## Getting In

Getting accepted to the educational program of your choice is next. Certificate programs typically have four requirements: completion of prerequisites, application submission, tuition payment and space in the class. Once these four elements are met you basically pay the money and go.

College degree programs are a different story. Admissions departments develop complex procedures for reviewing, sorting, considering and selecting applicants for the next class. Many undergraduate programs offer admission to more than half of individuals submitting completed applications. However, some highly selective programs—especially graduate programs—offer admission to as few as one in ten applicants. Your challenge is to make sure your application is in the "admit" pile.

Let's say you are on track to submit your application well ahead of the deadline. Good. Your past grades and test scores are what they are. Hopefully—good. You are a model of the success characteristics identified by the Higher Education Professionals Survey described in Chapter Three. What more can you do to increase your chance of being accepted? How can you help the admissions committee understand what a good fit you are for their program?

The answer—connect with the decision makers. What is important to them? How can you help *their* program succeed? Are you an interesting person who would add depth to the student population? Do you have leadership skills to contribute to student organizations? Does your life experience tell a compelling story of how you came to pursue this degree at this time; a story worthy of marketing material if you succeed? Why will you be a better choice than the other 50% of applicants (or 90%)?

Making a positive mark on the admissions committee takes more than a good story about how you would benefit from them; it takes equally good reasons why they would benefit from you. Most applicants will spend their time writing, speaking and asking questions about how the program will benefit themselves. These are important questions for the applicant and should be asked. But prospective students who focus only on their own needs waste an opportunity to truly market themselves to the school.

Four opportunities to make this connection are the personal essay, personal interview, reference letters and the special needs letter. Each is a chance to attach a story with your name. Each piece can build on the others to create a picture of who you are and who you can be as part of College X's student body. Simply stated, you are considering buying them; now it is time to convince them to "buy" (e.g., accept) you! Even if you have yet to identify how unique and special you are, think of the application process from a marketing perspective. Below are some suggestions for adding a marketing voice to your application.

### *The personal essay*

Nearly every application for a degree program requires a personal essay. Topics range from why you want to be a (fill in the blank) to how you overcame (a significant obstacle) to your philosophy on (some world issue such as immigration, economics or peace). This is your opportunity to tell a compelling story that leaves the reader wanting to meet the author. This does not require becoming a professional writer. Be yourself but get feedback from at least two people before you finalize the essay. Add specifics. At the very least, make sure spelling and grammatical errors don't disturb the flow of the writing. Leave the reader with images of you sitting in their classroom and you as a successful graduate.

For example, if your topic is "admission will fulfill my lifelong dream," talk about why. Show the reader how this became your dream, how you've held on to the dream and what you plan to do after graduation. Talk about real life experiences. Avoid film and TV references. Talk about your energy and interest in their program. Rather than saying, "I will lead student organizations," tell a past leadership story related to your area of interest.

The best story reflects areas of interest for the school and your targeted major. What is the school proud of? Do their marketing materials highlight student involvement in the community, global education, out-of-the-box thinkers? If your research about the program suggests they like creative types, include an example of when you creatively solved a complex or challenging problem. If they want caring types, talk about your volunteer mission work. If they want academic types, describe the affect a favorite professor or course had on your life. If you are still at a loss for topics or direction, a Google search on "college personal essays" yields ample resources for essay assistance and ideas.

### *The personal interview*

Personal interviews may be required or optional. They may be formal (i.e., with an admissions representative, department head, or alumni organization) or informal (i.e., networking with current students or alums over coffee). If the opportunity to meet one-on-one with a school representative presents itself, take it! Look good but avoid looking like a walking billboard for the program. Be prompt, polite, and send a thank you note.

Prepare a list of five good questions specific to the interviewer's role—and many more good answers for questions he or she might ask you. Good questions for an admissions representative focus on the academic program itself and what it takes to succeed as a student. Good questions for a program alumnus may include why they chose this program, what they wish they had known going in, and how the program benefited their career.

Well-crafted questions and thoughtful answers result in good information to include in each party's decision process. If you want to convince the interviewer you are up to the challenge of the program, ask the interviewer, "What are the biggest challenges for students with my background?" The answer provides data you can use to demonstrate why these are not challenges for you. Alternatively, ask the interviewer to describe a student who was very successful in this program. What separated the student from others? What was the key to their success? The answers will give you insight to what it really takes to succeed; and what admissions is looking for in an applicant.

### *A few sample questions to ask the interviewer:*

- What does a successful candidate for admission bring to the table?

- How does your program differ from others in this field? (Note: you should have done enough homework to know the basics; this question seeks subtle differences not described in the college brochure.)

- Have you had other students with my background come through the program? What are they doing now? Would it be possible to speak with one of them?

*A few sample questions they may ask you:*

- Tell me about yourself. Why you are interested in our program?

- Describe a challenge you overcame?

- What do you see yourself doing in five years? (Yep, this question is still around.)

- How does your background fit with this new interest?

- Give me an example of when you had too much to do and how you handled it. (Listen carefully to whether the interviewer says, "and how you handled it" or "how you accomplished everything." The latter is looking for how you get everything done whereas the former is about balance and prioritization.)

*The personal reference*

If required, reference letters should be requested from:

- People who have witnessed your success in settings that required comparable personal skills and characteristics (typically former instructors or managers).

- Individuals most likely to have credibility with the school's decision makers (Mom doesn't count even if she is a Fortune 500 CEO).

- Those who write well and follow directions, and most importantly

- People who meet deadlines.

The world's best reference source is useless if he or she is a sloppy writer, fails to follow protocol established by the program to which you are making application, or doesn't get the reference in on time. Unfortunately, the components of items three and four can be the most difficult to know when selecting references. Submitting your part of the application ahead of the deadline allows slush time in case you need to nudge your references a bit.

### The special needs letter

As each of my four children began the college search this single, middle-class mother working two jobs wanted her children to have the same educational options as their well-to-do classmates. Without funds or time to facilitate extensive research and travel, the application process had to be efficient and targeted. At the heart of this process emerged a document referenced by friends and family as "the $10,000 letter."

Traditionally known as the special needs letter this document is often mentioned in tiny print on financial aid applications. It is the applicant's opportunity to elaborate on the stories behind their data. The primary tone of the letter, from my perspective, is to help the decision makers see how this applicant is worth $10,000 or more *to them*—as a direct result of the life circumstances from which the applicant comes; the special life circumstances that make it impossible to pursue higher education without substantial financial assistance. It is a one-page marketing piece written by an individual who knows the applicant best; for myself and my kids that meant me.

I approached each letter as if the information might actually be worthy of $10,000 in near-term financial aid or in the long-term value of the degree being pursued. And to be clear, I made this number up. It was simply the amount I needed to believe was possible in order to summon the motivation to write a worthy statement.

Whether written by a parent for their child or by an adult for him or herself, there is a subtle but important difference between a financial needs letter that recites bills and burdens and the $10,000 letter. The first says, "We/I deserve," the second says, "You could have." Make sure what you write is in fact what they want. Think like a marketing executive. The stunning wildlife photos you took at age ten may not matter to admissions, unless you are applying to an art program. As you write, ask yourself, "Does this school actually care about this accomplishment?" If there is any question in your mind, find the answer or cut it out. Match what the school wants to what the applicant has. Save the rest for the holiday letter.

As it turned out, I'm convinced (rightly or wrongly) that each time I wrote one of these letters, it did indeed result in $10,000 or more in some combination of loans and grants. Given our financial situation (including years with multiple students in college), the letter may have had minimal influence on the amount of funding received. Yet, an individual I coached who had a low six-figure salary and an unexpected health crisis received a $3,000 grant in direct response to information provided in his letter. Others have received more. To me, the effort was worth the potential benefit.

I'm also convinced these letters add color to an application. School officials gain a deeper understanding of the individual within the context of his or her current life. Insights may be carried into the admission and financial aid decision by creating an image of how the applicant as an active student in the program.

Below are excerpts from a letter written by a Dean of Admissions and Financial Aid.

"I am writing to thank you for the wonderful letter you wrote…. I have added your remarks to [the] folder to be read by our Committee on Admissions as we continue our evaluation of our candidates. I very much appreciate the additional insights…. There is no doubt that your perspective can add a special dimension to all of the other information in our files. Our decision letters will be in the mail by the end of March. In the meantime, please know how much we value your contribution to our admissions work and how grateful we are for your letter."

Sincerely,
Dean of Admissions and Financial Aid

Finally, from a personal perspective, writing the letters gave me the chance to pause and truly appreciate the accomplishments and personal characteristics of each child—and of myself as I drafted a letter to attach to my own application.

## PSYCHING YOURSELF UP FOR SCHOOL

Move ahead a few months. The acceptance letter arrived. Financial and logistical pieces are falling into place. Schedules are being adjusted. Whether the road has been short and easy or long and challenging, the final days before your first day of class often include a mixture of excitement and apprehension. Like the bride who gets "cold feet" the week before her wedding, many returning students wonder anew if they've chosen the right school, the right degree, the right time. Will returning to school cost too much money, add too much stress on family and friends, or be more work than they can handle? The list goes on.

By this point you have put significant thought into each step of the path that led you here. Now, take a deep breath and do whatever feeds your confidence. You can do this. Rather than re-hashing your decisions, use anxious energy to lay groundwork for the next stage—life as a student. Here are a few tips from those who have gone before.

### Prepare to Study

Returning to school involves lifestyle changes. Nowhere is this more apparent than when it comes to one's study requirements. Late nights are more likely to be spent with unruly homework than with social events. Weekend adventures may require planning around exam schedules. Morning coffee money may be diverted to purchase extra study materials. Yet, good study habits promote academic success and reduce stress associated with being unprepared for class.

Set aside regular time and a physical place for effective study. Kitchen tables may look inviting but are often the center of family activity. You may be able to read the Sunday paper while carrying on a conversation interrupted by questions and phone calls with the TV blaring in the background, but studying organic chemistry may take a bit more concentration.

When considering physical location options, a good test is to ask, "Could a restless baby sleep here?" If no, determine what needs to change. Don't be surprised if family members don't understand why you can't read while they watch TV and ask intermittent questions (and maybe you can). If the necessary change is too hard on others or too difficult to enforce, find someplace outside your home that works. Libraries are a good option for many adults. Do you study best late at night or early in the morning? Perhaps you need music or silence. Food or no food. Whatever works for you, find it.

### New Resources for Support

Family and friends may or may not serve as your primary support when it comes to school challenges. These folks may be overwhelmed by added household or childcare responsibilities while receiving less of your personal time and attention. Plus, few adults are truly interested in hearing the details about school bureaucracy, frog dissection or some professor's grading practices. When possible, save family and friends for the issues that relate to them. Ask them to back your decision to miss your cousin's graduation party in order to study for exams. Request use of the reliable car for Thursday evening class. Thank them for not complaining when you bow out of holiday cookie baking traditions.

Locate others in your new academic environment that can help you through school challenges. Understand the role of various administrative departments such as career services, academic tutoring, library services and the dean of students. Identify student and professional organizations that are relevant and useful to you. Keep in mind that many professional organizations offer student memberships and conference discounts.

Talk to your classmates. They too have made it this far and are eager to succeed. Attend informal gatherings designed to give students a chance to meet. Start a study group. Exchange email addresses so you can help each other if one of you misses a class or has a question. In the process you may find a professional networking buddy or even a lifelong friend.

### Plan for the Unexpected

Whether returning to school for career renewal, personal growth or some combination, this adventure is primarily about you.

84

However, there are times to sacrifice study hours for the benefit of those closest to you. Perhaps your son is receiving an award at the state capitol, or your best friend asks you to be her maid of honor at her wedding, or your boss needs you to make a presentation at the next board of directors meeting. These are one-time events with specific dates that are fairly easy to accommodate, even during finals time.

Other events require a week, month or semester of time and attention. Weddings, work, family concerns, mental or physical health issues; whatever arises, take time to consider your options. These are times to carefully choose what activities truly require your attention. Ask for help. Think long term. If you need a short break, speak with your professors or the dean to see what options are available. If you need to skip a semester, think about how you will keep motivated in the meantime so a break doesn't become an end.

What if you are faced with personal tragedy? Personal tragedy diverts emotional, physical and spiritual resources—and rightly so. How or whether to put school plans on hold depends on the intensity of the crisis and its effect on you. Talk to the dean of students and your professors. These professionals can walk you through your options and guide you to other resources on or off campus. Resources may include academic counseling centers, support groups or another student who has had a similar challenge.

Several stories come to mind from my own school days. Following his son's tragic death in a preventable worksite accident, a fellow student gained conviction to finish a law degree and advocate for workplace safety. Another classmate struggled successfully in the face of multiple challenges including the unexpected arrival of a homeless, mentally ill uncle in need of heart surgery. A third put her dream on long term hold when her child was seriously injured in an accident that took the life of his father. Yet another chose to continue school after being diagnosed with a fatal illness. Three years later her obituary spoke of her good work as an attorney. She lived her dream, even if it only lasted a short while. Each student balanced his or her own goals with their present reality. Each chose a road they felt represented the best decision for themselves and their loved ones at the moment. Each was a success to themselves, family and society.

As you go forward give yourself the freedom to push pause or to let go if needed for a family emergency or simply for a mental break. You got this far. Your motivation and energy will take you where you truly want to go. Trust yourself. Your decision will be right for you.

## FINAL THOUGHTS

Congratulate yourself! If you are this far, you have clarified your educational and career goals; found, applied and been accepted in a program to help you reach that goal and possibly even made it past the first semester jitters. Good for you! The next two chapters of this book talk about how to enjoy the journey and stuff you can do while you are in school to ensure a successful leap to your new career.

# CHAPTER FIVE

# ENJOYING THE JOURNEY

*"Value learning in the broad sense
and the specific learning will follow."*

**R**eturning to school is a great adventure. Rewards and challenges will occur whether your course of study takes nine hours, nine months or nine years. You will meet fellow students with like-minded goals who walked similar paths to this program; one or more of whom may become lifelong friends. Taking time to smell the roses can be hard to justify when you are faced with the realities of work, school, and family responsibilities. Give yourself permission to take breaks along the way to appreciate this amazing journey. This is *your* journey.

This chapter presents words of wisdom gathered from those who have taken and enjoyed this journey.

## FINDING WORKABLE ANSWERS FOR YOU

Perhaps the most useful motto for the returning student (besides "this too shall pass," more on that later) is, "Do what works for you." Only you know the magic combination for your past achievements. Only you know the realities of your current life situation (which may change along the way, sometimes hourly). Or perhaps it feels like even you don't know what will work best for you.

The back-to-school experience is packed with decisions. Is it better to take courses taught by professors I like or courses that fit my preferred class schedule? Should I do an extra paper to get an A or spread the time between other studies and family? Would it help me get

a job after graduation if I quit my current position and studied full-time? The only 100% correct answer to each question is, "it depends." It depends on many factors, some under your control, many others less so (e.g., graduation requirements, family crisis, your own personality, the economy).

Study style is a perfect example. Embrace the methods that work for you no matter how different it is from anyone else's approach. What works for one person may be the worst possible option for another. Likewise, a successful study approach one semester may be a disaster during another (sometimes related to a change of personal circumstance, professor, or topic).

Some people study during class; others need dedicated hours of silence. Some buy every available study aide including tapes, workbooks, CDs, and flashcards; others choose one or none. Some take copious notes, outline in rainbow colors, and tab each section. Others don't.

Likewise, there are times during school to take a big risk and other times to let an opportunity go by. Will studying abroad for four weeks be worth the money and stress on work and family? Should I quit my job to take an internship for half my salary if it might turn into full-time employment after graduation?

Few returning students have the same freedom to take risks as the eighteen-year-old college students being funded by Uncle Sam or Mom and Dad. However, this is still a time for growth. Give yourself freedom to explore. When tough decisions come up, look at your situation, make a choice, and learn from it.

The best decision is the one that will help you reach your goal (keeping in mind that your goal may include non-school factors such as keeping your job or not permanently alienating your entire family). When the answer is unclear, talk to a couple trusted friends and then go with the decision that provides you with the greatest sense of peace.

Keep an eye out for new ideas but hold them up to the lens of your life. Some of the most useful techniques I learned for surviving graduate school came from classmates. Likewise, some of the worst techniques also came from classmates. The difference was whether or not I considered their technique in light of my personal situation. When I did, I chose wisely.

## Exercise: What worked for you?

Imagine your post-graduation party. The big question on everyone's mind is:

"How did you do it?"

Today, right now (stop reading at the end of this paragraph), write down your answer. Start with the answer on the tip of your tongue no matter what it is.

Next, list your top five reasons, and then your top ten. There are no right or wrong answers. Just remember this question is about HOW, not WHY, you went back to school.

1.
2.
3.
4.
5.
*Pause for thought*
6.
7.
8.
9.
10.

How did you make it? Was it personal drive, family support, tutoring centers, stellar organizational methods, walks by a lake, meditation or faith, brute-force studying, Sunday date night, take-out food, the unconditional love of a pet? Something else? Some combination? Don't worry about complete sentences or spelling. Just write.

Save this list. Take it out a few days before graduation. Next to the original list write your post-graduation insights of how you *really* did it. Include personal qualities that may have emerged during this time such as perseverance, creativity, ability to study efficiently, or willingness to prioritize and let go of less important things (dusting comes to mind).

You may or may not be surprised by your post-graduation answers. But for today, nurture your original answers because they represent what you believe will help you achieve your goal. Be ready to let go of habits or techniques that aren't as helpful as you hoped.

Most importantly, be ready to welcome new answers that appear along the way and make all the difference at just the right time. A study partner's memorization technique gets you through a hard class. Your brother's old sweater keeps you warm so you can concentrate in cold classrooms. The computer your family purchased as a "good luck in school" present travels with you to every class, study session, and exam. You can't imagine going through school without these gifts.

In addition, surprise resources for guidance and encouragement frequently show up in unexpected places. Examples include a respected professor who becomes a mentor/friend, a heartfelt picture from a small child, or a deep reserve of personal strength that emerges in the midst of challenge. Taken together, this is how you made it. Your task along the way is simply to notice and say thanks.

## COMPETE ONLY WITH YOURSELF

Competition is a part of life. Yet there are choices. Knowing when to compete and with who can make a world of difference in one's stress level and in the outcome.

For instance, competition with oneself can be productive. Choosing a minimum grade point average you hope to achieve provides motivation and direction to your studies. On the other hand, deciding you must graduate first in your class sets you up for constant self-comparison with every other student, a practice that is rarely compatible with enjoying the journey. In addition, pressure for perfect grades can make a bright student feel dumb and disheartened when he or she gets a B on an assignment.

If you feel extreme pressure to get perfect grades, review your primary goal for the degree. Chances are your overall goal is successful course completion followed by employment. Yet every program seems to have a handful of students for whom being number one is a primary goal ("Now that I'm in, I'm going to beat the pants off everyone."). Don't worry about them. Set your own goals and you will enjoy the journey, even if one goal is to finish with a 4.0 grade point average.

Be prepared as friends, family, and co-workers make unfortunate statements that contain intended and unintended messages of comparison and competition. "But Mary finished her program in only eighteen months." "Bill took six years to complete his degree so he still had time for his kids." "Isn't your family suffering with you being so busy?" And if that isn't enough pressure, students invite their own stress by comparing test scores and course grades. Do not do this. Seriously. Not only is it stressful, it is inaccurate.

Only if you lived in someone else's head, heart, and home could you have enough data to accurately compare the effort/outcome ratio of your grades to theirs. Sick kids, visits from relatives, relationship break-ups, furnace failure; as a returning student there is so much more of regular life that plays into a final grade than brute intelligence or effort. The same goes for how long it takes you to complete a program versus someone else. Don't use real life to make excuses but do allow yourself space when needed.

Academic competitions are another consideration. While it is a fact of academic life that certain awards and honors are determined by excellent achievement or grade point average, your approach to individual situations is a personal choice. Most academic competitions fall into one of two broad categories: Competitions you are automatically entered into, and those you must actively enter.

Competitions you are automatically entered into include class rank groupings (e.g., top 10%), dean's lists, some merit scholarships, and best-in-class awards given by a professor. These competitions occur no matter what you do. If you are enrolled, your performance is included in determining the winner(s). You have no choice in terms of having your performance judged, but you do have a choice about whether you want to 1) actively pursue the prize, or 2) do your work and let the chips fall where they may; in other words, not worry about it. Review your end goal and current life situation, and then decide which choice is right for you at this point in time.

In contrast, competitions you must actively enter are frequently competitions in a specific field. These require an application or audition. The competition may be based on individual achievement (e.g., art, music, writing) or team achievement (e.g., mock trial, construction competitions, math team competitions). Many schools have information about competitions for scholarship funds.

While it may be tempting to go after free money, especially if others are being successful, this is an ideal time to reflect on the phrase, "Know thyself." Ask yourself if this is the best use of your time, right now. Is the money really free? What is the cost to apply in terms of time and energy? How will the application process affect other studies, your work, or home responsibilities? Try to get a sense of the size and quality of the candidate pool. Can you earn an equal dollar amount in the same amount of time it would take to apply? If this is a chance for you to participate in a well-known competition or to merely gain practice competing then go for it. But if you feel guilty not entering because others think you should, and you imagine yourself being overwhelmed if you do, then don't. Listen to yourself.

## THIS TOO SHALL PASS

School is full of opportunities to practice perspective. Everyday details of life can appear overwhelming when there are demands from every angle. My favorite assistant dean for a weekend law program keeps a "This too shall pass" sign prominently posted in her office (and a box of tissues). She provides a hopeful and calm perspective for students learning to juggle work, family, and the rigors of law school. Through past witness to success and failure she helps students find answers and options that have been overshadowed by the passing struggles of the day.

This is a time to learn about you. An opportunity to reflect on the big picture of your life and what really, truly is most important to you. Likewise, it is a chance to reconfirm and build known strengths while uncovering skills and abilities you never knew were there. When it feels like every minute of your day is spent meeting the demands of an ever-increasing list of responsibilities, take a step back. Hold off on major decisions until the end of the semester, or at least twenty-four hours.

Pull out the personal statement you framed in Chapter Three that describes what you want out of this experience. Take a moment to recall the original feelings and motivation that brought you this far. Then remember: it is OK to change goals, take a break, or simply regroup. As Annie said, "The sun will come up tomorrow."

## BE YOUR OWN BEST FRIEND

One final thought on how to enjoy the journey: treat yourself as you would your best friend. Each returning student brings his or her unique set of circumstances and personal approach to this adventure. When hard courses or life's challenges throw you a rough semester give yourself a break. Congratulate yourself for hanging in there. Encourage your soul by taking a walk, playing your favorite music in the car or looking at family pictures. Visit a pet store. Go fishing. Buy chocolate.

If it is finals time and you can't take a break, study by a lake, or at least a window. Plan a special event after you complete a big project. Plan little events during the week. Invite a family member to meet you at school for a meal. Buy yourself flowers at the farmer's market. Choose not to vacuum this week. If you still feel troubled, get together with a best friend. Share your concerns and worries. Listen to his or her perspective.

## WHAT'S NEXT?

The next chapter of this book looks beyond graduation. Once you have the piece of paper in hand and new knowledge in your head, how do you make the leap to a new or enhanced occupation? Chapter Six describes activities you can do starting today to ensure your leap is successful.

# Chapter Six

# Making the Leap

"People cannot stay in the same job for their entire adult life."

The final step in the back-to-school journey happens after graduation. The sacrifices and hard work are now put to the test as the new graduate leaves the academic world, diploma in hand, intent on realizing an occupation-related goal. He or she is ready to make the leap to the new field.

As you well know, today's work world thrives on networking. Many opportunities never reach a job board but are filled by someone who knew someone who works in the department. This chapter begins with suggestions for building professional connections in your new field before you start school, while you are in school, and after graduation. The middle section describes mistakes that can derail a new career before it begins, and how to avoid them. Chapter Six ends with a look at one final element in the back-to-school journey—faith.

## BUILDING CONNECTIONS

Whether you are entering a new field or expanding an existing career, it is essential to connect with the professionals, clients, and culture of your target environment. Building connections along the way expands your professional network and increases your sensitivity to cultural nuances that spell success in your field. Having a good feel for the culture and clientele gives you a leg up over others who lack this knowledge. No matter where you are in your academic journey, opportunities are available to build these connections and prepare you for the final leap.

### Before Starting School

One of the best ways to connect with people working in your area of interest is to spend at least twenty hours as a volunteer. Volunteering gives you a realistic preview of the work itself and introduces you to the personalities in a specific field. When the match is good, you gain a mentor to answer questions and guide you along the way. And if you hate the tasks associated with the job, there is time to step back and look for a more compatible area of study.

A number of graduate programs require applicants to have prior experience, paid or volunteer, in the field of proposed study. For example, several top-notch MBA programs require applicants to have two or more years of business experience as a prerequisite to application. A Midwest health care program requires applicants to complete 100 volunteer hours with a certified professional in the proposed area of study. Each student in these programs comes to school with a common vocabulary, a sense of how coursework applies to real life on the job, and one or more connections to professionals in the field. Share experiences and contacts with your classmates. This is networking at its finest.

If extended field experience is not possible, seek out small-scale opportunities. Perhaps you could shadow a recent graduate for a day. Locate three professionals in your area of interest. Invite each for a low-key information-gathering lunch or coffee. Identify professional associations in your area of interest. Review their websites, look for conferences in your area, and read job ads to get an idea of what will be expected of you upon graduation. Applying one or more of these suggestions can jump-start your professional network and confirm if this field of study is, in fact, a good fit.

## During School

Most of the formal opportunities to make professional connections are available only while you are a registered student. Internship, practicum, residency, co-op job, clerkship, and apprenticeship are a few of the titles used to describe these programs. Some individuals return to school in order to gain access to these opportunities as a means of entry into a new field.

Many schools have placement coordinators to connect students with paid or unpaid options. A few programs sponsor on or off-campus clinics where students provide reduced-rate services to the public under faculty supervision. Clinic services range from hair styling to health care, legal services to car maintenance. Schools differ on the details of these programs. Ask experienced classmates what programs they found useful and why.

Alumni networking events are another great way to connect with professionals in the field. As a prospective peer and alum, these individuals are motivated to see you succeed. The success of each new graduate enhances the school's reputation in the community—which benefits all graduates.

Talk to your school's career services office. They may offer group networking events or one-to-one introductions to professionals in your area of study. Take courses with a hands-on practical emphasis. Look for a volunteer or part-time job in the field. Take advantage of student memberships in professional associations and deep discounts to conferences.

Given a bit of creative thinking, there are ways to build connections and experience before graduation day, no matter how hectic your schedule is during school. When it is time to make the final leap, you will be grateful for this groundwork.

## After Graduation

The moment you receive your diploma you become a member of the graduates' club. As such, you carry the title of alumnus and are considered a new professional in your area of study. Although some student-only doors are closed, others are now open—forever.

First, join the local and national professional organizations for your chosen field. If you were a student member, you know which they are. If not, Google "trade and professional associations [your field, your state]" to locate the relevant group nearest you. These are your new peers. Ask about new member benefits such as networking events, mentorship programs, job boards, and introductory discounts. Attend conferences, workshops, and trade fairs to learn about trends and topics on the minds of the pros.

Another good resource is the alumni association for your school. Networking with alums is unique because of your common bond of coursework, classrooms, and perhaps even professors. Credibility and encouragement come more quickly from those who have walked in your shoes. Further, the better each grad does in the marketplace, the better the reputation of the program, and the better it looks on one's resume. Many alumni groups maintain a Facebook or LinkedIn account in addition to hosting local face-to-face programs or networking events. Whether you connect in person or online, this is a great way to meet people who made a similar leap. Who knows? They might be looking for someone just like you—or know someone who is.

Finally, stay in touch with classmates. Serve as resources for each other as you build your networks and careers. These individuals have an inside view of the personal effort it took to complete this program. They also share your vision for success in your chosen field. Years from now, you may be surprised at the important role a classmate or two played along the way.

## PITFALLS AND DEAL-BREAKERS

Abby graduated with top honors. Her networking skills are superb. Her appearance is meticulous. And she can't get (or keep) a job. What is going on? This section explores common missteps that can derail your next career journey before it begins.

### Saying Goodbye to Grandma's Rocker

A popular software program depicts a pioneer family's journey to settle the west. Reaching the Promised Land requires careful attention to detail to remain on the trail. You need to find food and overcome illness. Savvy travelers soon learn that the first step for survival is to make careful packing choices for the journey. There is only so much room in a covered wagon and a lot of stuff various travelers wish to bring along.

In particular, items such as Grandma's prized rocker represent treasured memories of the homeland, especially if Grandpa's initials are carved into the chair. Unfortunately, Grandma's rocker can't be eaten nor can it serve as ammunition to catch a rabbit (which rarely move slowly enough to be bopped on the head). The rocker can't provide the warmth of a blanket unless used as firewood, and then only as a temporary fix. In short, Grandma's rocker takes up a lot of space that could preclude packing essential items. It is the big, heavy thing that weighs you down, draining energy and resources for the journey.

Major change, corporate or personal, often includes some version of Grandma's rocker. Maybe you finally purchased the snowmobile you've always wanted—two months before being transferred to Hawaii. When the company refuses to pay for shipping to Oahu you actually wonder if you should move. For some, Grandma's rocker is an old practice that individuals refuse to let go of. One customer service clerk continued to create hand-written file cards for each customer interaction years after the office was automated. More frequently, the metaphorical rocker is found in attitudes and beliefs carried forward in spite of ample evidence of impending doom.

Think about a successful leap or change in your life. What could have gotten in the way but didn't? How was "Grandma's rocker" identified? How did you make the decision to leave it behind? How did you say goodbye?

Below are common "Grandma's rocker" attitudes that can be the death knell for a new career.

*Demanding your highest prior salary in your first (new) job.* Let's be realistic. Rarely will past experience grant you an entry position where you left off. It took time to reach your highest salary in your prior career. It is going to take time in your next career. Relevant work experience may increase the speed of your climb up the compensation ladder, or it may not. No matter how annoying this is, don't let salary demands derail your transition to a productive career. Take a tempered view of initial salary expectations. Once you are in a job, build a network of co-workers and peers who see your value to the company. An initial willingness to take a cut in salary, title, and prestige in order to get a good start can lay a foundation from which to meet or exceed earlier compensation levels (if that is your goal) in a few short years.

*Expecting to be treated as an expert because of your experience.* Another common fault is to think you know more about the job than younger but more experienced co-workers. You don't. Not in this context. Not yet anyway. Before you can truly bring the value of prior experience to a new venture, you must first build relationships of trust and respect.

*Relying on workplace success techniques from your prior career.* The skills that brought success in your first career may not be the best today, especially if your first career began prior to the birth of the World Wide Web (recently itself declared an obsolete term). For example, more attention and time were allowed for problem-solving and perfection-seeking before the internet provided twenty-four-hour access to people and resources. Post-internet years saw product development cycles cut in half and half again. Highly qualified individuals from the "old school" were replaced by less experienced workers ready to balance acceptable quality levels with deadlines. To what do you attribute your career success in the past? Now sit down with someone thirty-five or younger and compare notes. You will both walk away richer.

*Harboring first career ghosts.* This is a new day. Take what you learned from the first career but move forward with new eyes. Look out for these annoying ghosts:

- *Old complaints and grudges.* Bringing old beefs into a new situation robs you of the opportunity to experience something different. It also irritates the heck out of those around you.

- *Romanticized images of the prior career.* This ghost can create an impermeable wall between you and a new opportunity. Rather than saying, "At Company XYZ we always did this [not that]" say, "What about this as an idea?" Stories that reek of good-old-days mournfulness get old fast. Before long your colleagues only hear, "This one day, at band camp…" (*American Pie*, 1999).

- *Cultural assumptions.* This ghost is more subtle. Culture is the essence and personality of an organization. It colors every choice and every decision. It underlies a company's

100

approach to meetings, project management, people management, problem-solving, break practices, dress, corporate acronyms, and definitions of success. Talented professionals can hit a brick wall if they fail to learn and respect the culture of their new organization.

As you prepare to make the leap to a new or enhanced career, what do you believe must come along? Use the following chart to make a list. Next to each item summarize why this is essential? What does it mean to leave it behind? What is the cost for leaving it behind or bringing it along? Is there a compromise or other possibility? Moving potential roadblocks to the side can lighten your load and save months of back-breaking nonproductive work.

## Essentials for the Journey

| What do you feel must come along? | Why is this essential? | What does it mean to leave this behind? | What is the cost for bringing this along? | Possible compromises; other thoughts. |
|---|---|---|---|---|
| | | | | |

## WHAT'S FAITH GOT TO DO WITH IT?

Leaps, especially really big leaps, involve preparation, courage, strength, and faith. You've been preparing for this leap since you first thought about returning to school. You demonstrated courage through the many difficult choices you made to complete this degree. You showed strength beyond imagination when there was

101

more going on in your life than anyone could possibly know—and you still passed a difficult course. You graduated in part because all along, you had faith that it was possible. You had faith that you could do it. You had faith in the process and in yourself.

Faith is belief that is not based on proof. As such, faith differs from belief. Beliefs often include a form of "if this, then that." Andy believes Sara will complete her part of the project because she always has. Manny believes his parents will visit over the holidays. Finnegan believes he must take his medication to stay well. Beliefs include a sense of guarantee or at least a test for validity. Beliefs feel rational. The assignment is due. Either Sara has done her part or not. (Check) Manny's parents arrive on time. (Check) Finnegan stops taking his meds and becomes ill. (I thought that might happen.)

Faith is bigger. Faith is more than hope but less than human certainty. Faith embraces trust, confidence, letting go, doing all you can and then expecting that things will work out, somehow, someway.

Belief is when the shy seventh grader takes his best shot from the free throw line, confident the ball will go in the basket. Faith is what happens when he closes his eyes, takes a deep breath, shoots and is still confident. Picture all the leaps you have made to get this far. Recall times when the path was less than clear, moments when your best talents or plans were insufficient, times when you had to trust in your preparation and just go for it—and you did.

Relatively speaking, you are about to do something that a very small portion of the world's population has even tried. Perhaps it is a tiny voice in your head or a loved one's loud voice in your kitchen, but somehow you have come to have faith that all this will be and is, in fact, possible.

Recall the months or years leading to the decision to return to school. For many adults, the leap to becoming a student again is a hugely significant, personal leap into the unknown. You know the basket is there but can you hit it without a clear line of sight? Yes. You did. The leap to your new field is equally possible.


## MOVING AHEAD

The final chapter, Travel Stories, is a collection of narratives written by grownups who returned to school. The individuals represent five decades in age, come from many walks of life, and represent an amazing variety of starting points and personal motivation to return to school. This is my favorite chapter. When you need inspiration, read a story or two. They made it. So can you.

# CHAPTER SEVEN


# TRAVEL STORIES

"I have learned anything is possible."

Chapter Seven compiles personal stories shared by individuals who returned to school between the ages of twenty-eight and sixty-three. Each individual carried adult responsibilities into the classroom, although circumstances leading them back to school varied. For some, returning to school fulfilled a lifelong dream. For others, it was merely the next step in a well-traveled life.

Whether the result was an exciting new career or a deep sense of personal accomplishment, each story describes a journey that uncovered a new world for the traveler. Their stories speak of hope, courage, perseverance, reaching beyond comfort zones, and having fun. You'll read about a woman who was the first in her family to graduate from high school and is well on her way to earning her bachelor's degree—as a single mother with a full-time job. You'll read about a man who achieved an early dream to attend law school, after his career was cut short by an accident. Writers include individuals who are still in school as well as those who graduated years ago.

The storytellers were asked to share their back-to-school experiences using the following questions as a framework. They were not required to answer each question, nor were they confined to this list. Creativity was encouraged.

1. **Describe your beginning.** What motivated you to return to school? Were you working? Have family responsibilities? What was your biggest concern?

2. **Highs and lows.** What were the best times for you as a returning adult student? What was the biggest challenge and how did you deal with it?

3. **Surprises**. Looking back, what were the things you least expected (good things and challenges)? What information would have helped you navigate the challenges?

4. **Outcome**. Was returning to school a good decision for you? Why or why not?

5. **Best tips.** To what do you most attribute your success? What words of advice do you have for those considering this journey?

6. **Anything else?** Is there something you'd like to share with those considering returning to school that wasn't covered in the other questions?

7. **Inspiration**. Please include (and cite the author) any favorite inspirational phrase, motto, or image that kept you going through difficult times.

The stories are presented here just as they were submitted by each author, with the exception of minor edits. As such, each traveler's voice can be heard through his or her words. Only first names or, when requested by the writer, pen names, are given to maintain a minimal level of anonymity. The exception is the husband and wife stories of Howard and Marika Stone, founders of 2 Young 2 Retire (www.2young2retire.com) **and authors of the book**, *Too Young to Retire: 101 Ways to Start the Rest of Your Life.*

One final word about legacy. No matter what your motivation is for going back to school, know that you will leave footprints for others to follow. The stories in this chapter are a testament to that fact. Your journey matters. Your legacy starts now.

# Joyce B. – Unfinished Business

*Age when returned to school*: 45 and 51

*Area of study*: BS in Finance and Educational Psychology, MBA

*Age at time of writing*: 56

*Position today*: Director of Treasury. I handle cash and investments for a $2.5 billion dollar health insurance company. In addition to that, I work on strategic planning, Board reporting, and special projects.

### What motivated you to return to school?

I always regretted never finishing my degree. I had been working for a privately held company for eighteen years. When it sold, I was offered a job by the new owners but felt it was my opportunity to go back to school and finish my four year degree. I graduated two years later (2000) and then went on to get my MBA in an executive program from 2004 to 2006. I did my MBA to prove to my kids it can be done. I would love it if they would follow in my footsteps, only a few years earlier.

### Were you working? Have family responsibilities?

For the first year of my undergrad experience, I worked as a consultant. I realized I could finish sooner if I took a year off, so I did. I took twenty-six credits over the summer, nineteen credits in fall, fourteen credits in spring, and had my BA. My MBA was designed for working adults, with classes every other Friday and Saturday with a few full weeks, so yes, I worked during that program too. I started my undergrad program when my son went off to college (he claimed that I wanted to finish before he did) and my daughter was fifteen.

In retrospect, it was very hard on my daughter because I was not the most attentive parent. When I went for my MBA, my children were both out of high school.

## What was your biggest concern?

When I started, success; later, finances, time, and sleep!

## Highs and lows

In the MBA program, I really enjoyed the interaction with people from different companies, who had different titles and experiences. It opened up my world, not only on a business level but a personal level as well.

The biggest challenge was going from being the go-to person at work to not knowing anything. The perfect example was taking calculus after not having taken a math class in twenty-five years—I had forgotten everything!

## Surprises

The amazing friends I got out of the deal, business opportunities I never expected, and the satisfaction of completing my education. Challenges—asking for help (a new paradigm), total exhaustion, dealing with difficult people or those who did not contribute on group projects.

## What information would have helped you navigate the challenges?

The undergrad part definitely helped me with the MBA. It was much easier for me to admit I needed help or did not understand. I was much more prepared for the work load I knew was coming, and was faster to understand how the group dynamics would affect my work load.

## Was returning to school a good decision for you?

Are you kidding, it was the best. It made me portable. I could never have my current job without that piece of paper. It increased my confidence and expanded my possibilities and awareness.

## To what do you most attribute your success?

Hard work, perseverance, and tenacity.

**What words of advice do you have for those considering this journey?**

DO IT! It is very tough but well worth it. I got my education in my area of expertise so when I went job hunting it really increased the jobs offered to me and the compensation. Sticking with what you know gives you a lot of bang for your buck.

**Anything else?**

I think the most important thing is to have someone in your corner—it can get very difficult and it is very different from the work environment. Have someone to encourage you as you move along.

**Inspiration**

I have no idea who the author is but I quote it often. "It is not the things you do in life you regret, it is the things you don't do." I am really glad I "did" this.

# Julie L. – A Look to the Future

*Age when returned to school:* 26

*Area of study:* Bachelor of Science in Nursing

*Age at time of writing:* 31

*Position today:* I work in a local hospital as a nurse extern where I get hands-on experience working under a nurse preceptor.

## What motivated you to return to school?

I was motivated to return to school because I couldn't see myself in my current career much longer. I was twenty-six-years-old, and I couldn't imagine working at my job when I was twenty-nine, let alone sixty or sixty-five. I was working as an entry-level chemist. I was married, and my husband and I were hoping to have a child. When I got pregnant, the feeling to return to school increased. When my son was born, we moved back to my home state. I couldn't find any job in the chemistry field. That made the decision even easier.

## Highs and lows

The best times were the excitement of starting the program and then completing each term and feeling closer to my goal. The biggest challenge was leaving my son at daycare. My husband was working, and I also worked part-time. The amount of time I spent in class, doing homework, and working, turned out to be more hours than a regular full-time job. I felt awful guilt. To get through it, I just kept reminding myself that it was temporary. Nursing school was only three years long, it wouldn't be forever.

### Surprises

Honestly, I didn't expect to feel so old! As a chemist, I had always been one of the younger people at work, and was often the youngest. When I went to school, all of these nineteen- and twenty-year-olds looked at me like I was somebody's grandma. They seemed to feel awkward talking about things like parties in front of me, as though I might somehow disapprove or chastise them. I don't know if any information would have helped me navigate this ahead of time. I just needed to make sure I kept a good sense of humor. It was pretty funny.

### Was returning to school a good decision for you?

I believe returning to school has been a great decision for me and my family. The flexibility of nursing will, in the long run, enable me to spend more time with my family. I will be able to make a decent amount of money even if I only work part-time until the children are older. I can work three days a week in a hospital, or I can make my own schedule doing home care. It seems like the possibilities are endless!

### To what do you most attribute your success?

I really attribute my success to staying positive and my family. It's really tough to keep positive when you feel like the worst parent in the world because your child is always crying for you, you can't seem to keep your house in order like you used to, and you feel like you never see your spouse. It's definitely a sacrifice, but like I said, it will be better for me and my family in the long run. In this economy you just have to 'do what you have to do.'

The other thing I contribute my success to is our family—primarily my parents, my husband's parents, and my sister-in-law. They have been willing to babysit while I study for an exam or go to class. My mom has even cleaned my house a couple times while she watched my son when I was at clinicals. I could not have done it without their help.

### What words of advice do you have?

Don't be afraid to ask people for help. And accept some of your limitations. It's tough to compete with young people that don't have families or jobs. They might have a lot more time to devote to school than you do, and you just have to accept that as reality.

## Inspiration

What inspired me were my son, my husband, and definitely feeling like I needed to do something to make our lives better. The other thing that really inspired me was getting scholarships. At the end of my first year, I was feeling pretty low. Nursing school was tough. I wanted to spend more time with my family. I was also scared. What if I couldn't do it? What if I could only get so far, and then I didn't make it? Look at the sacrifices we all had made! Money was a big issue, and so I applied for scholarships. And then I actually received some!

The fact that other people, strangers, could look at me and my background and information and believe in me enough to help me pay for my education—that really made me think. I know I am strong, I know I am smart, and I know I can do this. If those other people who don't even know me, if they think I can do it, so much so that they help me pay my tuition, that really did inspire me. It made me feel that other people were pulling for me too; not just myself and my own family, but my community was pulling for me as well. And I know I can make a difference in my community as a nurse, so part of me feels like I am doing it for my fellow citizens as well.

Good luck!

# Larry M. – Accidental Journey

*Age when returned to school:* 50

*Area of study:* Law

*Age at time of writing:* 54

*Position today:* District Court Law Clerk. I'm responsible for managing courtroom details such as jury coordination and filing of motions and orders. I also write judicial orders, findings, and memorandum, and provide legal analysis to assist in judicial decision-making.

### What motivated you to return to school?

I worked in advertising and marketing for many years, owning my own business for the last seventeen years. Then my wife and I were hit by a truck that ran a red light. My wife was left permanently disabled and I lost the use of my right arm for six months until they were able to restore it through traction. In the meantime, I lost my business and had to start over.

An elected official for whom I had been the campaign manager hired me as a policy aide. About the same time, I was elected to my local school board. Working daily on policy matters for the state and setting policy for the school district reminded me how much I had enjoyed my business law classes as an undergrad thirty years earlier. The classes were taught by a law professor and were very comprehensive. I had toyed with the idea of law school after completing my BA. But, I was married and we were ready to get on with life, so I went to work.

I worked the entire time I was in law school, was married, had one daughter in Notre Dame and one across the street at St. Mary's of Notre Dame. My two sons were older than the girls and married;

one the father of my two granddaughters. My biggest concern was to stay engaged in my family, keep my job, and get re-elected to the school board. Two out of three ain't bad. I was defeated in the next election; it's hard to campaign when every minute is consumed with family, work, and study.My other concern centered on whether or not I could still do what I had to in order to compete with the younger students who had more time to study. I was able to balance work family and study, finish a 4½- year program in 3½ years, and still end up with a 3.16 when I graduated. It's not cum laude but the top half works.

### Highs and lows

Education is definitely wasted on the young. It is a ball to go back to school after experiencing the reality of life. And, to know what it's like to buy a house and a car, to run a business and to set policy was an ideal foundation for my course of study—law. The biggest challenge was learning that, as an adult student with work, family, and other commitments, I wasn't going to be able to do it all. I had to learn to prioritize what was important and try to do the 90% while letting the 10% slide.

### Surprises

I have to say the thing I least expected was to find so many friends and close relationships among the students. A lot of these kids were younger than my oldest son and yet we studied together, ate lunch, and commiserated after finals. The biggest challenge was to stay attached to my family. The best advice I got was from a friend who told me to take one evening off a week as date night. It helped me stay connected to my family and my wife.

### Was returning to school a good decision for you?

Oh yeah! The joy of learning, especially when you're over fifty, really sharpens your mind. Even with all of the pain, stress, and hassle, I would do it all over again in a snap.

### What words of advice do you have for those considering this journey?

Perseverance. Don't give up.

# Kathy W. – I Can Do This!

*Age when returned to school:* 48

*Area of study:* Associate of Science—Individualized Professional Studies degree (leading to a bachelor's degree in Chemical Dependency Counseling)

*Age at time of writing:* 50

*Position today:* I am currently a student, housewife, and volunteer.

## What motivated you to return to school?

I have a passion for learning new things! I am a member of a twelve-step program called Al-Anon. At open speaker meetings, I heard how others made a decision to go back to school later in life in spite of difficulties. Many had dropped out of high school (I did, too), and now have a master's degree! I was very impressed! I thought, if they can do it, I could too!

I decided to go back to school after being laid off from work. I am married, have no children, and felt it was the right time. My biggest concern was not being able to remember things after being out of school for thirty years! I found, though, that I could always take notes.

I always loved a challenge. I had very little computer experience. I was able to take some beginner adult computer classes on the side through my local workforce center. I found out there were many others who had little computer experience. I was not alone!

## Highs and lows

The greatest time was when I registered for an adult learning program at my college called the ASAP program (Adult Success through Accelerated Program) at Inver Hills Community College in Inver Grove Heights, MN. I was forty-eight years old! This is an amazing two-part class that helps you design your own degree. They have accelerated classes that you can take, and prior learning competencies that you can arrange to complete with help from their instructors. You work at home on your own for these competencies and meet with an instructor to go over your work. You get a pass or fail. If you pass, you receive the credits for that class. I received thirty credits in competencies from prior learning experience! It was great!

My biggest challenge was dealing with the deaths of family members and several friends during my first two years in college. This spring and summer alone, I lost my last surviving aunt and my brother. I knew I had to remember what I was taught in the adult learning program. We were encouraged to tell ourselves something positive in the mirror every day. Every morning I looked in the mirror and told myself, "I can do this!" I am determined to succeed. I know my brother and aunt would be proud of me.

### Surprises

The thing I least expected was that the younger students would be so understanding. Many told me they had a mom my age. Yet, I still felt young being in class. It was so fun! I did not feel old at all. Going to class invigorated me and helped me stay focused. The challenges were that I have fibromyalgia and a connective tissue disease which acts like lupus. Many nights I do not sleep well. I asked questions about flexibility and was able to fit my schedule accordingly. I learned not to take on too many classes at once. I took early start and later start classes in the semester, which helped lighten my workload of homework during any one time.

### Was returning to school a good decision for you?

It is the best decision that I ever made! This is the greatest gift I have ever received! I feel so blessed to have this opportunity to shine in a field that I have such great compassion. My goal is to get a Bachelor's degree in Chemical Dependency Counseling, and then get a master's degree in Psychology. I did not have a chance to go college years ago, as my parents both died within a year of each other when I was eighteen. I always wanted to go, and this has been the most rewarding experience of my life!

**To what do you most attribute your success?**

My success started with taking the adult learning class at my college. I learned many valuable tools, which helped me learn how to set priorities for myself when going back to school. I learned a lot about time management and not to take on too much at once, which many of us as adult learners do. By taking this class with other older students, I found out that I was not alone. They shared many of the same fears and questions that I did.

**Anything else?**

When I first started class, a younger student noticed how hard I was working at taking notes. He asked me if I would like a little tip to do well. I said, "sure." He told me to not procrastinate…to work on my homework a little every night, always turn my work in on time, do extra credit, and study hard for the tests. He said, "If you do that, you will do very well." He was right. I listened to what he said, and I am doing better than I ever dreamed possible!

**Inspiration**

"I'm not quite where I want to be, but I'm not where I used to be, I'm headed where I'm meant to be, and I know God is watching over me." (Author Unknown)

# Deborah P. – Terms of Healing

*Age when returned to school*: 40

*Area of study*: Master's in Library and Information Science (in my 20s), master's in Human Development (in my early 40s), and associate degree in Nursing (in my late 40s).

*Age at time of writing*: 60

*Position today*: Senior Program Manager, nonprofit organization for healthcare research and education. I manage a variety of research, education, and outreach initiatives aimed at making healthcare more integrative, holistic, and healing for patients, professionals, and society at large.

### What motivated you to return to school?

I was working part-time as a librarian and had two young children. I was involved in childbirth education and interested in approaches to healing and well-being such as meditation, guided imagery, and music. A friend had just finished a master's program that gave her a lot of latitude in finding advisors and coursework that met specific professional needs that she had.

So twenty years ago, I remember exactly the spot where I was walking when it hit me that I could do this too! I could take all the childbirth work and healing studies I'd been doing, integrate and take them farther, through this same very creative master's program—*Wow!* So that's what I did. My greatest concern was my on-again-off-again ability to stay focused and on track. It took me almost five years to finish the degree, but I loved doing it.

As I was finishing that program, then of course I wondered how I was going to apply all of this new learning. Over lunch, a close friend, a nurse-midwife, said the fateful words to me, "Deb, bite the bullet. Go to nursing school." It was a light-bulb moment. I knew that a nursing degree was what I needed to apply the master's work.

This time my concern was about the sheer magnitude of the challenge. Nursing school is demanding and intense. I was a working mom. Whatever would this be like?

## Highs and lows

In the master's program, the high was the opportunity to do some real exploring, creative thinking, and writing. The greatest challenges were time and focus. I just stayed with it, on my own schedule, and finished. The nursing program held some absolutely wonderful things—realizing how much I enjoyed the science of it; being with patients, not just as someone carrying out procedures, but as a present, observant, and caring person; the opportunity to teach fellow nursing students about the use of breath and sound to help patients relax and center; and bonding with others who were going through the boot camp of nursing school along with me. Challenges never quit. It is, rightly, a demanding and intense program. Learning happens constantly on every level—mental, emotional, physical, and spiritual. It is a workout for the whole human being. Fundamentally, I survived because I had an unbudgeable commitment to figuring out how I was to be of use for the well-being of others. And I survived with the support of my husband, some of my wonderful nursing student colleagues, and a very dear friend and nurse-mentor.

## Surprises

I was pretty realistic in approaching these programs. I quit a number of things that had been important to me, including community theater involvement and teaching childbirth classes. Friends who had been through this program made clear to me what I was facing in terms of work and stress. That didn't make it easier, but it did mean I wasn't surprised.

There was one negative surprise. Perhaps it was because I went back to school in my forties, after a twenty-year professional career, teaching experience, and being a mother, but I didn't expect to find any instructors who were demeaning or small-minded, but there they were. There was a "feminist" psychology professor who believed you could only be a feminist if you were exactly her sort of feminist. And there were a couple of nursing instructors—one who

120

was notoriously rude and harsh, and another who was probably the worst teacher I've ever had. If I'd been younger, I might have taken this poor quality of teaching for granted. As a middle-aged person, I had higher standards and found it annoying to be "learning" from people like this.

## Was returning to school a good decision for you?

Without question, it was the right thing for me to do. I wasn't on a life-sustaining path in my previous work. I had done whatever I wanted to do as a librarian, and some kind of new life was calling. I didn't know what that was—in some respects, I still don't—but setting out on the path was and is without question the right thing for me to do.

## To what do you most attribute your success? What words of advice do you have?

I'm someone who does well in school. The structure and community are supportive for me. Beyond that, what got me through was a strong desire to integrate different kinds of knowing—mental, emotional, spiritual, and physical—and a commitment to finding out where all this was leading. It's the "why am I here?" question. In all the hard work, I listened to my intuition. Listen for your passion. What feeds your heart and your vitality? Going back to school isn't easy, but if it serves what's most deeply meaningful to you, you can do it.

## Inspiration

Driving to my nursing classes and clinicals, I listened to recordings of Gregorian chants composed by twelfth-century abbess Hildegard of Bingen. Her music soothed and balanced me. Hildegard also wrote medical texts, so I felt aligned with her. She comforted and inspired me.

# Renee C. – For My Daughter

*Age when returned to school:* 25

*Program of Study:* Associate degree in Health Information Technology; bachelor's degree in Business Administration

*Age at time of writing:* 31

*Position today:* As a Program Officer, I oversee the Bay Area Community Foundation's scholarship programs working directly with students, schools, donors, colleges, universities, staff, and committees to ensure scholarships are awarded based on established requirements. I also lead the Youth Advisory Committee's grant making, fundraising, and volunteer activities.

**What motivated you to return to school?**

I graduated high school in 1996 and was the first person in my family to do so. I thought that I was ahead of the game just getting my high school diploma. I had great job opportunities—I got into Consumers Energy and then GM Powertrain making very good money. Of course, it was only a matter of time until I was laid off like everyone else. I attended a local community college on and off during my time at GM because it was recommended AND they offered tuition reimbursement. I thought after being laid off, with my extensive experience at both previous jobs, I would be able to find something. I was laid off for two years.

The day I found out that my daughter was coming into the world I made myself a promise to go back to college and not take any time off until my degree was completed. Although I really wanted to at times, I have not even taken a spring/summer off. I am starting my fifth year of being a single mom, working full time, and going to college. I want to be the best mother and role model possible. I want to give her things I never had—not material things but certain experiences and opportunities. Not that my parents were bad parents—they were amazing. They had me at a very young age and worked their butts off to give me everything I needed—they are my heroes and my best friends. My biggest concern is paying off my own student loan so I am able to help my daughter pay for her college. I am hoping that all the effort, time, money, and stress will pay off when I finally have my bachelor's degree.

**Highs and lows**

The best thing about being an adult and returning to college is the feeling of self worth. As time goes on I am more confident in myself and truly amazed at what I am able to accomplish in a short amount of time. I have learned how to save time; even by minutes here and there. I have to; otherwise I won't have time to sleep. Which brings me to the challenges—balancing life is very important. I need quality time with my daughter and my family. I have to teach myself pretty much every subject since I have to take all online classes to save time for work, household duties, etc. I log on to school after my daughter goes to bed at night.

**Surprises**

I surprise myself by attainting good grades and finishing classes I never thought I could pass. I learned that all instructors are different and expect different things; make sure that is clear right away. Most instructors at my college are willing to be flexible with students because they realize that most all of the students there are working adults with many hats.

**Was returning to school a good decision for you?**

I believe it has been a good decision so far because of my confidence level as well as the expectations of moving up in my current position. Hopefully, after I graduate, I will get a raise to assist me in paying off the student loans I have accrued.

**To what do you most attribute your success?**

My daughter—she is my inspiration. I have learned anything is possible—you just need to see it, say it, and believe it.

# Donald S. – First Calling

*Age when returned to school:*  46

*Area of study:*  Master of Divinity, Luther Seminary

*Age at time of writing:*  50

*Position today:*  Following a one-year internship serving a rural community of five churches, I'm working in the seminary dining hall as I finish the final year of coursework.

### What motivated you to return to school?

When I was fifteen years old my social studies teacher asked each of us in the class what we were planning to do for a career. I surprised even myself when I answered that I want to be a pastor. Shortly after that declaration I discarded the idea because I didn't think I was a good enough person to be a pastor, so I tried other things like being a radio announcer, a machinist, a boat builder, and for twenty years I was an optician.

Still, I had the nagging feeling I wasn't doing what I was called to do as a human, so I had a chat with my pastor and discovered that God really wanted me to be a pastor after all, so I enrolled in seminary at the age of forty-five. I had a good job as an optician; my sons were finishing high school and headed for college. After a tumultuous marriage, heart-wrenching divorce, and a couple of years of self-rediscovery, I had just gotten remarried. I wondered if this was really God calling or a mid-life crisis, and I wondered if I could afford to go back to school while trying to maintain a relationship with my sons, since the seminary I planned to attend was 1,500 miles from where they live.

124

## Surprises

Once I enrolled in seminary as a "second-career student," I discovered there were many people my age and even older who were feeling the exact same things I was. Getting to know them helped support my decision. We commiserated as we struggled with the foreign language requirements of studying Greek and Hebrew, and supported each other as we discussed how difficult it was to maintain family relationships and engage in the discipline of study. Forming study groups and support groups with these peers was invaluable during the first few semesters of study.

When I declared my intention to enroll in seminary study to my friends at church I was surprised at how supportive they were. When I announced that I was going to Luther Seminary, suddenly there were people who wanted to help pay my tuition and some even gave me books, along with money for books, to make sure I felt supported in my decision. Since I had promised my younger son that I would remain in the area until after he graduated from high school, I had to learn how to navigate online classes, but with the help of some friends who were familiar with online environments, this proved to be a challenge that was easily overcome.

## Was returning to school a good decision for you?

I have felt nothing but positive about my decision to return to school. I have no regrets about leaving the optical industry, and I look forward to many years in my new career as a pastor. It has helped that many people have supported my decision, including my sons, and it has also helped that I have had some opportunities to work as a pastor in some churches to discover if this is what I am truly called to do.

## Words of advice

One thing that I would advise others who are considering a career change is to look for online classes and feel encouraged to take them. Online learning offers flexible scheduling so that it is possible to continue working at a job that pays well while still going to school. It is easier to maintain family relationships when the class schedule is flexible enough to meet your own schedule. Don't feel pressured to complete a course of study in a particular time frame. Work at a pace that is manageable rather than trying to do too much at once.

**Inspiration**

If anyone is feeling miserable in the work they are doing, they are probably doing the wrong work. As Frederick Buechner wrote, "One's calling in life is that place where your deep gladness and the world's deep hunger meet."

# Mother and Daughter - For the Love of Learning

## Jean W. (mom) – Leading the way

*Age when returned to school*: 33

*Area of study*: English teacher

*Age at time of writing*: 82

*Position today*: As a "Lady of 80" I keep the home fires burning and take charge of our finances. Having traveled the world, we're content to be at home, read books, listen to music, or watch a video. We are enjoying our retirement that we planned for so long ago.

### What motivated you to return to school?

Having always enjoyed school, I graduated from high school in 1944, in the top ten percent of my class. Since I had taken college-prep courses, my parents anticipated that I was going to college. Instead, I married at seventeen and started a family. (The war, you know.)

At the first opportunity, I took college extension classes at a nearby high school. I was also teaching music in my home and knew that I enjoyed teaching. By the age of thirty-three, feeling the need for college and seeing the possibility, now that my children were in junior high, I enrolled in a small liberal arts college as an English major. Finishing my studies in three years, I started teaching at the high school.

### Highs and lows

Just being on campus was exciting. Combined with the joy of learning and the feeling of personal growth, it was an exhilarating experience. Challenge: setting priorities, scheduling time.

**Surprises**

This pertains to graduate school. After a few years of teaching, I saw the opportunity to work as a librarian in the new high school being built. I quickly took a year's leave of absence and enrolled in the graduate library program at the university—only to find that one of the classes was taught at night to accommodate those teachers attending part time. That caused a serious problem with transportation, since the last bus from downtown Cleveland left at five o'clock. My dear husband drove to the campus those nights to pick me up (a fifteen-mile round trip) having already driven a sixty-mile round trip to his own job.

**Was returning to school a good decision for you?**

Returning to school was the best decision I ever made. It changed the course of my life. It made all things possible. Of course, it meant sacrifices for the family but ultimately, they benefitted, too. We were able to enjoy a higher standard of living, including travel.

**To what do you attribute your success?**

I attribute my success to the love of learning, self-discipline, and the loving support of my husband who was always there for me. Advice: If you're really motivated, do it, or you will always have regrets.

**Anything else you'd like to share?**

There's no need to feel trapped in your situation. Take one hour each day to prepare for your own future. I took my children to the library and read to them. Moreover, while they napped, I treasured that time for my own reading, mostly nonfiction. Be prepared for the future.

**Inspiration**

Reading biographies of successful people inspired me. I particularly enjoyed biographies of women, like Marie Curie, who overcame many obstacles to achieve great things.

# Rosemarie J. (daughter) – Keeping options open

*Age when returned to school*: 29

*Area of study*: Nursing

*Age at time of writing*: 64

*Position today*: I retired from my full-time nursing position in 2005. Today I work on a contract basis for the same hospital's employee health department. This allows me to work when it is convenient for me leaving unlimited time to travel and to pursue my watercolor painting.

## What motivated you to return to school?

In 1967 I graduated from a three-year diploma program in nursing. In 1974 I was living next door to the university where my husband was a graduate student. They offered a Bachelor of Science in Nursing (BSN) program, so I thought—why not return and get my BSN. I was working full time as an RN in the emergency room at a local hospital and had a five-year old son. My initial concern was affording tuition although the hospital reimbursed some of my tuition each quarter.

## Highs and lows

The best times were enjoying what I was learning and the feeling of accomplishment. The biggest challenge was finding time for everything: working full time (we needed my wages to live on), finding time to study, to write all the required papers, to do the visits to many community agencies, home visits to care-plan clients, not to mention any family time or to be involved in my son's activities.

### Surprises

The biggest surprise was the amount of time school required of me. And that took time away from my husband and son. Had I known this in advance I might have postponed my classes until my husband had his graduate degree and my son was older.

### Was going back to school a good idea?

Earning a bachelor's degree was a matter of personal accomplishment. My BSN did not increase my earning power as a staff nurse. I did not have a desire to go to graduate school, but if I had, a BSN would have been essential. I graduated in 1977 at the age of thirty-one. I had the knowledge that many avenues of opportunity were open to me if things changed in the future. I never felt trapped in a position for lack of a degree.

### Best tips

For anyone married with children and a job, it is essential for the entire family to have an understanding of the time the returning student will need to study. The other parent will need to spend more time with the children, doing household chores, etc. I was eventually able to go down to a part-time position at work while in school, therefore gaining extra time which was a precious commodity.

### Inspiration

"You must do the thing you think you cannot do."

– Eleanor Roosevelt

"Never, never, never give up."

– Winston Churchill

# Gary J. – The Gift of Opportunity

*Age when returned to school*: 55

*Area of study*: Associate degree leading to bachelor's in Organizational Leadership

*Age at time of writing*: 56

*Position today*: After many years in the workforce, today I am a full-time student.

### What motivated you to return to school?

After thirty-five years in the printing and graphic arts industry my position was eliminated due to the economic downturn. Along the career transition path I discovered a simple question in material from a job support group: "Do you have an educational plan?"

I wondered how to locate a resource to answer this question. I learned that a local community college was participating in an upcoming job fair. Going to the job fair was daunting; the table for the college had a pamphlet about an accelerated program for adults returning to school. I picked up the material, returned a post card, and made an appointment with the program Recruitment Coordinator. At our appointment I concluded that not having a BA degree was impairing my career transition, and without it the journey would be longer and less rewarding.

I committed to attend my first college course in over three decades. The outcome would be an educational and action plan to earn my bachelor's degree, the solution to my original question. I was willing to pay the tuition but was pleased to learn the first class was paid for by a grant for returning students. I tried to be patient for our first class meeting in two months. My motivation to return to college is to earn a BA degree to improve my career opportunities!

**To what do you most attribute your success?**

Seek out and be open to good information from many places. In a local organization whose mission is to listen and encourage people experiencing transition, I found a place for broad and positive thinking about change. I was asked, "Are you looking at least five years into the future for training in occupations that may not exist today?" This encouraged me to think long term. Later, my son's psychology professor introduced me to general systems theory and systems science. This theory fit with my broad view of organizations, how they develop and how people interact as part of a community, and sparked a new vision for my future. Finally, in a conversation with the coordinator for my initial class, I discovered she, too, had been influenced by this theory of organizational learning and that the instructor for the class I was waiting patiently to start was trained in this science as well! At that point I knew clearly that I was in the right place.

**Highs and lows**

It is not a casual thing to decide to go back to school for over two years to complete a bachelor's degree in your middle fifties. You want to make it right, perfect, meaningful, achievable, and sustainable; no matter what you choose, it will be challenging.

The first class lasted six weeks. We covered many areas of learning, took personal and career assessments, studied qualitative and quantitative research and analysis, and discussed planning, action, and evaluation. There was a lot of thinking, reading, writing about our learning. We networked, met with instructors, spoke with our families and developed an individualized implementation process. It was an active time. I wanted to get the most I could from the learning. It seems I have a lot of catching up to do!

In addition, unemployment is a difficult time for anyone, no matter what stage of their life it occurs. I have been given a tremendous opportunity and the gift of time to respond. I have spiritual health, physical health, a very supportive family and circle of friends, old and new. I have met people and done things that I would not have done while being employed and am truly grateful for all these things. I have heard poetry and heard people speak on topics I thought would have no influence in my life, only to realize that their poetry and material was needed and necessary at that moment. The wealth of new ideas and learning has at times been overwhelming. I have experienced new emotional highs and lows, greater than at any other part of my life. This too has been part of the learning and discovery of self.

During that first class it became evident that I have the capacity to achieve my goal. Based on my new interest in systems theory, my assessments, my resume and work history, my writing, and our conversations, our instructor suggested that I visit a nearby university and look into their Organizational Development and Leadership degree program. As it turns out, this program is a perfect fit.

My fears about inadequacy, a complicated process for entry, or a long and meandering road through classes were soon dispelled. The university offered an evaluation of your transcript prior to enrolling. From this I learned there are five prerequisite classes I needed to take to start their accelerated degree program. One is offered as a regular class of sixteen weeks; four are eight week accelerated classes. This class structure is helpful because I want to transfer as soon as possible. The BA degree in Organizational Development and Leadership is an eighteen month course, forty-eight credits in fifteen classes, meeting once each week, and is cohort in structure, meaning the students who make up the class move through the program together.

## Anything else?

The journey of lifelong learning continues. I now know it should not stop, there are too many pitfalls in choosing to stop, and the people who pay the price for your not being a lifelong learner are those that you love the most. I consider this whole thing to be a total gift and incredible opportunity for me to go forward and do things in life that I would never have done.

# Sabrina S. – Beyond the Struggle

*Age when returned to school:* 31

*Area of study:* Associate in Applied Science—Diagnostic Medical Sonography

*Age at time of writing:* 34

*Position today:* Currently I work as manager of a car wash. I hope to locate a position in a hospital when I begin the clinical part of my program.

### What motivated you to go back to school?

My name is Sabrina. I am thirty-four years old, and a single mother of two beautiful children. My daughter just turned thirteen and my son is nine. As I was growing up, no one ever encouraged me to go on to college after high school. My parents were divorced when I was real young and neither have a college degree. I think this may be why they never pushed it on me.

I decided to go to college because I was sick of struggling. I wanted to be a good example for my children while being able to give my children every opportunity they deserve in their lives. I knew that there was no way I was going to be able to help them if I remained on the path I was on. So I started attending a nearby college in 2006 taking half-time credits. This was one of the most difficult commitments I have ever made. I remember many thoughts that raced through my head at that time—How am I going to pay for this?—How can I fit this into my already busy schedule? (Working full time, while raising two children, and picking up any odd jobs I could find to make ends meet.) It's been ten years since high school, can I still do it?

134

**Was going back to school a good decision for you?**

This was the best decision I have ever made. I have three classes left before I move into the clinical portion of my program. This was a rough journey, there were many times when I didn't know how I was going to get through this experience. I'm not finished yet, and I'm sure there are many hard times yet to come. I've made it this far and won't let anything get in my way now. In high school I didn't have the care and concern I have now, and didn't receive that good of grades. But college is completely different. I have maintained a grade point average over a 3.2 and made the dean's list repeatedly.

**To what do you attribute your success?**

I have many people to thank for this. Since I have gone back to school I have had an excellent support team of friends and family members. But the people I thank most of all are the donors who have made a commitment to the Bay Area Community Foundation scholarship program. There is one scholarship that helped support me every year since I started applying; that is the Zoe scholarship. I am so grateful for the donor and hope one day to be in the position to help someone else in a similar position to the one I am in now. This experience has given me confidence I didn't have before. It also helped me to see that there are still good people who do care in this world but you have to care and better yourself in order to experience this.

# Jeff H. – Something New

*Age when returned to school:* 29

*Area of study:* Master's of Science in Software Engineering

*Age at time of writing:* 37

*Position today:* I work with corporations as a Software Consultant. I work with business experts to draft requirements, conduct work estimates, design and build software.

## What motivated you to go back to school?

I was looking for a new direction in life and a new career. After trying out an introduction to programming class I knew it was something I would like. I worked full time initially while going to school part time, but then I saw that job cuts were looming, so I switched to full time student status just as the economy crashed in 2001. I was single when I started back to school and had no other family responsibilities so I decided to go full time. My biggest concern was getting a job when I finished the degree. I did get some resistance from my father who felt I should work throughout school. But in the end, I think I made the right decision for me.

## Highs and lows

I met a lot of people in my program. It was nice to have a large network of friends again. In the working world it seems like everyone slowly begins to lose friends and never really gets together aside from the odd weekend. School is much more social. My biggest challenge was mitigating the expectations of my research assistant faculty member. He seemed to think he could wave a magic wand and I would produce results!

136

## Surprises

I was surprised by the number of adults and the number of foreign students in my program. School wasn't as challenging as I had remembered. Knowing more about the industry I was transitioning into would have helped. But there is such a steep learning curve in this field I'm not surprised I didn't know more about the industry at that time.

## Was returning to school a good decision for you?

Yes. I tripled my salary in three years. Plus I enjoy my work immensely.

## To what do you attribute your success?

I worked very hard, very diligently, day and night for both years of graduate school. I humbled myself and listened to others. I didn't boast about my past career or really talk about it much at all. No one cares what you did or used to do. It is what lies ahead that's important. Focus on that. Don't look back.

## Inspiration

"Insanity: doing the same thing over and over again, expecting different results."

— Albert Einstein

# Husband and Wife are *2 Young 2 Retire*

## Marika Stone – From practice to professional

*Age when returned to school*: 57

*Area of study*: Yoga instructor

*Age at time of writing*: 60

*Position today*: Co-owner *2 Young 2 Retire*. I manage the website 2young2retire.com and write a blog of the same name. I also do public relations for our Unitarian Universalist congregation, lead Laughter Yoga groups, and make music with Howard.

### What motivated you to return to school?

I was coming to the end of a great run as a solo entrepreneur providing editorial services and speech writing to a Fortune 500 list of clients. The youngest child was in college and the nest was about to empty. I knew my next career would be in complementary health, so I followed my interest in therapeutic movement, hypnosis, and the like. I was already practicing yoga regularly, and one day the decision to pursue this professionally became obvious. My one concern was that perhaps fifty-seven was 'old' to start something so physical. But as it turned out, there were five others in my age group taking the training. I gradually gave up my clients as I started to teach in my home studio.

### Highs and lows

Best times: finding kindred spirits and community in yoga; good conversations; sharing what I was learning, and learning from others. Biggest challenge. Living away from home for a month; sharing a room

138

with a stranger; committing Sanskrit words and phrases to memory; 'getting' the yogic philosophy and adapting it to my own use.

## Surprises

I did not expect the program to be as physically and emotionally intense as it was. We had one half-day off in the first two weeks, and that was difficult. I didn't imagine I would be doing as much yoga and it took time for my body to adjust to that, but then, I really loved it. A manual about the training and what to expect re: housing, meals, rules, and what kinds of changes we might anticipate in our bodies and minds, etc., would have been helpful.

## Was returning to school a good decision for you?

It was the best thing I could have done and I wouldn't change a thing.

## To what do you most attribute your success?

Focus. Commitment to the process. Surrender. Once I make a decision, I am totally focused on and committed to following through. But I also realize that I cannot control the outcome and must to some extent, go with the flow. That is hard for me because I like control. My advice is to let yourself discover strengths you perhaps didn't know you possess. Allow surprises; find joy in whatever you do, even if it seems trivial.

## Anything else?

Don't get bogged down in details of a prospective program too soon. You want to make sure the choice is the right one for you, so spend enough time on that part. Once you know where you are going, the details seem surprisingly unimportant.

## Inspiration

"When you follow your bliss, doors will open where you would not have thought there would be doors; and where there wouldn't be a door for anyone else."

— Joseph Campbell

"You don't have to get it right. You just have to get it going."

— Mike Litman,
motivational speaker
and author

# Howard Stone – The hidden coach appears

*Age when returned to school:* 62

*Area of study:* Certificate in life coaching

*Age at time of writing:* 67

*Position today:* Co-founder *2 Young 2 Retire*; I am currently training/ certifying coaches, social workers, and other professionals to facilitate group conversations based on our book; ongoing personal transition coaching collaborations, leading Laughter Yoga groups, and playing/performing jazz.

## What motivated you to return to school?

At age sixty-two, at the top of my core career, I started feeling restless after our three children became independent and grandkids were on the horizon. I read about personal coaching in an in-flight magazine and began exploring the next chapter that would allow me to develop a service to others without the need to walk away from a satisfying and lucrative job right away. Making and spending money did not feel like enough. Money and health were both in fine shape, so the beginning of the transition was without major concerns.

## Highs and lows

Training with motivated folks of all ages at Coach University while engaged in a conversation that was mostly missing in the business world in 1997 was exhilarating. The biggest challenge, after knowing I was in the right place for my future, was discussing my transition out of the company with the owner. We agreed on a two year overlap.

140

### Surprises

I was surprised to learn that in some ways I had been serving others in a personal way throughout my life, and that that this new skill set was a formal extension of who I had already become. Feedback from colleagues and clients validated my natural talents to help others get more out of their lives.

### Was returning to school a good decision for you?

Yes. The 2young2retire website, book, coaching, and training business came out of it.

### To what do you most attribute your success? What words of advice do you have?

I knew intuitively where to go; that became crystallized with assessment tests and coaching.

My advice:

- Get a sense of your time and resource abundance.
- Get to know your signature strengths.
- Ask for help. Don't do this alone.
- Hang out with independent thinking, creative, and optimistic people. Realists will slow you down.
- Read and re-read this book and "Too Young to Retire: 101 Ways to Start the Rest of Your Life."
- Never introduce yourself as either a retiree or what your job title or profession used to be.
- Take extraordinarily good care of yourself.
- Enjoy the journey and laugh frequently.

### Inspiration

"The enshrinement of leisure is the worst poppycock ever perpetuated on the population."

> — Marika C. Stone,
> Poet, Yoga Teacher,
> Co-Author, *Too Young
> to Retire*

"Ships are safest in harbors. But that's not what ships are made for."

> — Dr. John Stephenson

# Laura G. – Grandma Goes to Law School

*Age when returned to school:* 23, 29, 41, 49

*Area of study:* Music, industrial relations, educational psychology, law

*Age at time of writing:* 55

*Position today:* Consultant, author, speaker, professor, attorney

**What motivated you to go back to school?**

Financial need was the motivation for me to return to school the first two times. Later, it was to fulfill a personal goal. The assumption is often made that I love school. This is incorrect. School is difficult and stressful for me. In high school I believed college was far beyond my ability. Still, I wanted to become a lawyer. Our small town lawyer was a central figure who helped people and businesses with problems big or small. I wanted to be that useful. Unfortunately, I was informed that women weren't allowed in law school (an unfortunate bit of misinformation.) So, after high school I chose a performance-based school where I knew I could compete.

The performance courses went well but the few academic classes were hopeless. I guessed on most tests. Halfway through the program my first child was born and I dropped out to reconsider my future. In the final weeks before my daughter was born I took a temp job. A female co-worker was a student at Harvard Law School. "How did you get in?" I asked. "There are five of us in my group," she said. "It isn't easy but we want to be attorneys."

During the next two years I looked for options to complete my bachelor's degree. After moving to a new city I discovered a college with a flexible schedule where I could work, study and take care of my growing family. Two years and three months later I received a

142

bachelor's degree in music, one month before my third child was born.

At the age of twenty-seven I divorced. The next three years of struggle proved that a musician's erratic pay was insufficient to provide the life I wanted for my children. At age thirty, as a working single mom of four, I went back to school again. Having an undergraduate degree gave me choices. A two-year master's degree in business won out over three years for law school. The extra money and time to complete that third year was out of the question. Plus I heard law school reading was really hard.

Over the next fifteen years I had a fine career in Human Resources. I loved helping people and organizations thrive. I especially enjoyed collaborating with employees and leadership to create healthy organizations. However, terminations and workplace conflict wore me down. A former professor encouraged me to return to the classroom for a PhD, this time to study how adults succeed or fail in the workplace. I thought of it as my self-defense doctorate. My master's courses transferred and my employer offered tuition reimbursement. I graduated in 1997 with two kids still in college and one in high school. Although the PhD didn't lead to a new career it opened a number of doors for me as a consultant and speaker.

In August, 2001, I was walking through the woods with a retired friend at adult band camp (yes, I still play music.) In the middle of our conversation he stopped me in my tracks and said, "I just have one question for you. When are you going to law school?" This gentleman was unaware of my ongoing interest in law. "Why do you say that?" I asked. He proceeded to give me a long list of reasons and declared "You must hurry because school is about to start." In 2005, as a grandma of two, I graduated with honors from law school.

**Highs and lows**

There were two distinct high points in law school. First, I established the Second Career Society, the first student organization at the school geared for working adult students. Second, I studied abroad. During previous back-to-school experiences it was all I could do to manage the kids, school and work. Law school was my first chance to splurge on me. I attended a short summer program in Ireland. It was the best thing I did as a student, academically and personally.

The low point was during the first semester when old feelings of not being smart enough cropped up. My adult children jumped in to provide the inspiration I needed to continue. They encouraged me to finish out the year no matter what. "You paid your money. You've always wanted to do this. Big deal if you flunk out. At least you'll know you tried." Each shared stories of their own college years. One son painted a picture with the Eleanor Roosevelt quote, "We must do the things we think we cannot do." My grandsons gave me study rocks from their collection. The painting and study rocks remain on my desk.

**Surprises**

I was surprised by the energy, can-do attitude, and mutual support among the second-career law students. We held full-time jobs and attended school each weekend. We were in way over our heads but we were in this together. We were intent on graduating with our families and personal lives intact. Study groups included ages and personalities that would not have mixed elsewhere. The life stories were amazing and inspirational. I found mentors and lifelong friends younger than my children. We survived and thrived because we worked together.

**Was going back to school a good decision?**

Yes. The bachelor's degree provided the foundation for a first career and allowed me to pursue graduate school when I needed to make a change. The master's degree was a valuable credential in the marketplace that led to good jobs and sufficient income to buy a home and help four kids attend college. The doctorate opened professional doors that required this credential. The law degree provided entry to an interesting career in data privacy law and brought closure to a personal goal.

**What words of advice do you have?**

First, never give up. Regroup, change goals, take a break, *choose* to let go, but never give up. Second, find friends at school who are different from you. Seek their perspective; start a study group, or gather for lunch. They will notice things you've missed. Third, keep your family and friends in the loop. Let them know how they can help and how much they are appreciated. Establish a regular time family and friends can look forward to that is all about them. Celebrate your successes and theirs together.

## Inspiration

"You must do the thing you think you cannot do."

— Eleanor Roosevelt

"Whatever you are, be a good one."

— Abraham Lincoln

## This page is for your
## BACK-TO-SCHOOL STORY

Now sit back and imagine yourself starting, traveling and completing this journey. Answer the following questions as you envision them today. After graduation, in your rediscovered free time, do this again. Then submit it to http://backtoschoolforgrownups.com with your contact information. You may be in the next edition ☺

*Name:*


*Age when returned to school:*


*Area of study:*


*Age at time of writing:*


*Position following graduation:*

1. **Describe your beginning.** What motivated you to return to school? Were you working? Have family responsibilities? What were your biggest concern?

2. **Highs and lows.** What were the best times for you as a returning adult student? What was the biggest challenge and how did you deal with it?

3. **Surprises**. Looking back, what were the things you least expected (good things and challenges)? What information would have helped you navigate the challenges?

4. **Outcome**. Was returning to school a good decision for you? Why or why not?

5. **Best tips.** To what do you most attribute your success? What words of advice do you have for those considering this journey?

6. **Anything else?** Is there something you'd like to share with those considering returning to school that wasn't covered in the other questions?

7. **Inspiration.** Please include (and cite the author) any favorite inspirational phrase, motto, or image that kept you going through difficult times.

# APPENDIX

## HIGHER EDUCATION PROFESSIONALS SURVEY

The *Back to School for Grownups* Higher Education Professionals Survey was conducted in the fall of 2009. A web-based survey was sent via email to approximately 300 professionals at institutions of higher education across the country. Recipients included college administrators and professors from institutions that have an established adult student population.

A total of forty-four surveys were completed during a ten-day period. Responses were anonymous unless the respondent self-identified. The academic positions held by respondents who revealed their identity provided insight and confirmation to the strength of opinions expressed in the data. Among these individuals are eight professors, three deans of programs targeting adult students, six deans or directors of admissions and/or financial aid, a state director of higher education, two library directors, a former law school dean, and a former college president; the latter two from institutions with established traditional and nontraditional programs.

All forty-four respondents answered Question 1. Thirty-five respondents expanded a "yes" response with their insights regarding the trend in adults returning to school (responses provided below.) Seven responses to the numerical portion of Question 2 and Question 3 were not usable. Consequently, the analysis of success and derailment factors described in Chapter Three is based on thirty-seven responses. Likewise, thirty-nine respondents provided information to Question 4.

**Question 1**: *Have you seen a growth in the number of adult students returning to school?* (N=44)

Yes     91% (n=40)
No      9% (n= 4)

If "yes," do you think this trend will continue? Why?

- I believe the trend will continue because undergraduate degrees do not hold the weight they once held. In order to be competitive in the job market, a student has to have an advanced degree.

- With the current economic situation the safest place to be is back in school.

- The economy, job losses, down-sizing, longevity all will contribute to the growth of adult students.

- I do believe it will continue, because adults are exploring second careers today; stepping out to try that 'new' challenge. They are also savvy about 'enhancing' their existing education/resume.

- Because people change careers a lot and this often necessitates retraining. Also because going back to school is often essential to remaining current in any career. I think returning to school is becoming the norm, rather than the exception.

- Yes, the economy and people living longer, productive lives will continue to "push" adult students back to school for retooling, training, and finding new, exciting career opportunities.

- Yes, as long as the economy is in bad shape adults will continue to go to school.

- Yes, due to the current state of the country and the desire to return to work.

- [The trend of adults returning to school] will continue because the life span is increasing, new skills are needed for encore careers, and the idea that learning has no finish line is spreading. The educated want more education, and want to meet other smart grownups.

- I think this trend will continue well into the year 2010, or as long as the unemployment rate remains as high as it is. Measured nationally at this time (September 2009), the rate of unemployment is 9.4%. In 1982, the national rate of unemployment was 10.2%.

- My opinion is unemployed persons will tend to return to school for more training during recessionary periods. I have noticed an increase in enrollment.

- It will continue for several years due to the poor economy.

- It probably will not continue to grow at the same rate— assuming the financial situation improves.

- The nature of work today demands new skills and knowledge all the time. Current skills become dated and new skills need to be acquired. Also, people become tired of the work they are doing and look to new careers.

- We have actually benefited from the slow economy that has driven many students back to finish their degrees in order to be in a more secure job hunting position.

- The need to significantly "re-tool" is only going to accelerate in the fast-changing world we find ourselves in.

- Yes, until the economy improves and they can find work.

- Yes. Learners want more specialization and more professionalism for their current careers, and to launch new careers.

- The economy has forced some to return to school to enhance their education and skills. Others express the need to "find more meaning" in their work and want to redirect their career.

- Changing economy necessitates career changes and additional credentials.

- Economy.

- People cannot stay in the same job for their entire adult life. Jobs change over quickly now with technology running our lives. Adults need to learn new techniques to stay current with the technology.

- I think the economy has driven many displaced or underemployed workers to community colleges. Many of them will continue on to a four-year institution to complete a BA degree.

- Yes, [due to] job layoffs.

- Yes. Career change, economy and market shifts, acceptance of continuous lifelong learning.

- There is a greater availability of programs designed to meet the needs of working adults.

- [Adults are returning to school] for job advancement, personal edification.

- The economy may be providing impetus for adults to return to school, particularly if they are currently unemployed.

- "Because of the need for new or additional education/ training of the workforce and adult literacy needs."

- This trend will continue as adults continue to train for an ever increasingly complex work world. Also, there seems to be more flexibility in the larger social consciousness around changing careers allowing people to seek more personally satisfying work.

- Right now the economy is placing students in the position of unemployed or underemployed. While that will change, the number of jobs people hold over a lifetime will continue to increase. That means more retooling as jobs shift in a global economy.

- The need to constantly improve one's knowledge and become more competent.

- At least in the short term, based on changes in the job market and economy.

- The recently unemployed are returning to college to finish degrees or to increase their hiring potential.

- Students are ready to learn more information.

**Question 2**: *In your experience, what are the three most common characteristics of successful returning adult students?* (n=37)

| THIS TABLE IS RANKED BY TOTAL "TOP 3" COMMON CHARACTER-ISTICS OF SUCCESSFUL RETURNING ADULT STUDENTS | | | | |
|---|---|---|---|---|
| n=37 | 1st Choice | 2nd Choice | 3rd Choice | Total "Top 3" Responses |
| Time-management skills | 6 | 3 | 7* | 16 |
| Perseverance | 4 | 6 | 5 | 15 |
| Commitment | 8* | 4 | 3 | 15 |
| Willingness to ask for help | 4 | 4 | 2 | 10 |
| Family support | 1 | 7* | 2 | 10 |
| Tenacity | 3 | 2 | 4 | 9 |
| Clear goals | 2 | 4 | 1 | 7 |
| Ability to "roll with the punches" | 4 | 1 | 1 | 6 |
| Self-knowledge | 1 | 0 | 5 | 6 |
| Ability to let go/be imperfect | 1 | 2 | 2 | 5 |
| Good multitasker | 2 | 1 | 1 | 4 |
| Perspective | 1 | 0 | 2 | 3 |
| Study skills | 1 | 2 | 0 | 3 |
| Sense of humor | 0 | 0 | 1 | 1 |
| "A" student | 0 | 0 | 0 | 0 |
| Other | (see list below) | | | |

*Indicates the factor that received the most votes within a specific rank. For example, "Commitment" was ranked most frequently (8) as the #1 cause of student success. However, "Time-management skills" received the greatest number of votes overall (16). "Family support" was not among the top three characteristics ranked by total vote, but was the most frequently ranked #2 characteristic.

*Other factors (Please specify)*

- Difficult to cull that one down to just three—The successful adult learner is a nearly equal mix of virtually all of these! Could not succeed without any one of them.

- Intellectual curiosity.

- Probably all of the above play into success.

- Patience with self.

- Willingness to work hard without assurance of immediate positive feedback.

- Life experience.

- High value on education.

**Question 3**: *Based on your experience, what do you believe to be the three most common derailers for returning adult students?* (n=37)

| THIS TABLE IS RANKED BY TOTAL "TOP 3" COMMON CHARACTERISTICS OF ADULT STUDENTS WHOSE RETURN TO SCHOOL IS DERAILED | | | | |
|---|---|---|---|---|
| n=37 | 1st Choice | 2nd Choice | 3rd Choice | Total "Top 3" Responses |
| Financial issues | 12* | 5 | 5 | 22 |
| Unexpected events | 4 | 9* | 8* | 21 |
| Family complications | 6 | 7 | 5 | 18 |
| Inability to persevere | 5 | 3 | 3 | 11 |
| Unclear goals | 4 | 3 | 3 | 10 |
| Technological inabilities | 2 | 0 | 7 | 9 |
| Poor study habits | 1 | 5 | 2 | 8 |
| Know-it-all attitude | 0 | 3 | 0 | 3 |
| Personal health | 0 | 1 | 2 | 3 |
| Perfectionism | 1 | 0 | 1 | 2 |
| Poor grades | 0 | 0 | 1 | 1 |
| Not open to new experiences | 1 | 0 | 0 | 1 |
| Generational divide with other students | 0 | 0 | 0 | 0 |
| Other | (see list below) | | | |
| * Indicates the factor that received the most votes within a specific rank. For example, "Financial issues" was ranked most frequently (12) as the #1 cause of student derailment. "Unexpected events" was most frequently ranked as the #2 or #3 most common reason for derailment. | | | | |

*Other factors (Please specify)*

- "Keeping busy" with trivial pursuits like entertainment, daily newspaper, bingo, etc.

- Changing lifestyle to adapt to student life.

- Self-doubt.

- Procrastination.

- First, the inability to add education to their already busy schedules. Second, finding low-cost childcare when they attend classes.

- In her book, *The Longevity Factor* (1993), Lydia Bronte states, "Creativity is not just the privilege of youth." This is a perceptive comment. Of course, accident or serious illness may interrupt anyone's effort to be creative and productive.

**Question 4**: *What one thing should adult students returning to school know?* (n=39)

- You are not who you were when you were last in school. It is important to be open to new challenges and self-understanding.

- Everyone there is just as nervous and insecure as you are.

- Relax...be able to take criticism and laugh at one's self.

- That the minute they start, there is a "light at the end of the tunnel." It's not forever. Take each term as it comes.

- This too shall pass.

- How to navigate the system to get what they need.

- It will go faster than you think, take time to enjoy the experience.

- You don't have to be an "A" student to be successful.

- They must dedicate time to study so that they can focus with minimal interruptions.

- Why they are there.

- They are capable of much more than they can imagine.

- Adults returning to school should not be afraid to learn new technologies. They should be willing to risk failure to learn and advance.

- Whether or not they are committed to changing their lives.

- Value learning in the broad sense and the specific learning will come along with the general things.

- That it is possible to return to school and excel; don't be afraid that young students will be so much better at it.

- Without healthy motivation, the task is near impossible.
- There is no perfect time to start back in school. Life will always be busy. The longer you wait to jump in, the longer it will be before you graduate!

- How to set up an effective personal network to help navigate the "system" and provide personal support.

- You won't be able to do everything you want to do since the coursework will take high priority. So pick the most important parts of your life to stay tied to.

- Age is not widely respected by the younger learners.

- This too shall pass—there is a start and an end.

- Even if their study habits are rusty, they will catch up quickly if they are willing to work hard and not get thrown by the changes that have taken place since they were in school.

- That everyone makes mistakes. Learn from them and move on.

- That "smart" is what you become when you are determined to learn and willing to ask for help.

- This is the time to prepare for that career you always wanted. Make the most of your time on campus. Use the resources, make connections; claim your education.

- You need to have a time commitment.

- Age and life experience is appreciated by most younger students.

- Access the resources available on campus to support your success.

- Support systems are available and professors are motivated by nontraditional students.

- While efforts will be made to offer courses at times/in ways that accommodate their busy lives, the curriculum or course requirements will not be modified.

- "You can teach an old dog new tricks.".Learning can be fun!

- How hard it is; but also rewarding in unexpected ways.

- Don't let your age or time away from school deter you from pursuing further education.

- In the process of juggling many important balls, school is not likely to be the most important. Usually, family is first, job/career is second, and school is third. It requires considerable tenacity and time management to keep the third ranked ball in the air.

- The excitement of learning with and from other like-minded students.

- Time management, including an emphasis on life balance, is key.

- They're in good company; many other students their age are already in the classroom.

- That there are so many services for students to enjoy.

- "To fully realize our potential as human beings and accomplish all that we are able, we must develop the courage to be imperfect."— Rudolf Dreikurs

## More About the Author

*Back to School for Grownups* was established in 2009 by Laura H. Gilbert, PhD. As a working wife and mother Laura returned to school to finish her formal education in music performance. Several years later as a single mother of four Laura went back to the classroom. Laura's passion for the adult learner grew as she saw the sincerity and tremendous effort put forth by many nontraditional students; often for the benefit of family members or others they hoped to serve. A natural collaborator, Laura connected students, professors and college administrators to one another through their common interest in student success.

Laura's careers include professional musician, human resource executive, attorney, consultant and professor. She has designed and led initiatives in organizational effectiveness, performance management, and training and awareness at all levels of the organization. Laura has coached individuals and families from initial higher education decisions through the school-to-work transition and career path planning. Today she also teaches organizational leadership to adult learners in an evening MBA program.

The book, website and materials are based on her personal and professional experiences returning to school and helping others do the same. Laura began her studies at the Boston Conservatory of Music in Boston, Massachusetts. She completed her bachelor's degree in music at Metropolitan State University in St. Paul, Minnesota. She later earned a master's degree in industrial relations and a doctorate in educational psychology with an emphasis on learning and cognition from the University of Minnesota. In 2005 Laura graduated with honors from Hamline University School of Law. Laura also holds professional certifications in human resources and data privacy. Laura resides in Saint Paul, Minnesota, where she divides her time among occupational, academic and family pursuits. Laura is available as a consultant, speaker, and coach to corporate and academic organizations, groups or individuals who are exploring the back-to-school journey.

Laura can be reached at laura@backtoschoolforgrownups.com.

Copies of several charts and tables from *Back to School for Grown-ups* can be downloaded and customized for your own use.

Go to the Tools tab at: http://backtoschoolforgrownups.com

Username: backtoschool
Password: ICanDoItToo! (case sensitive and includes the "!")